It is definitely

no coincidence that

you happened to find this book!

It is certainly **not by chance** that you

opened it to this particular page. Some-

where in this life there are ✳ **Miracles**

with YOUR name on them, and you are

now about to discover precisely

what they are and **how** to access

them with amazing ease!

Be the change
you want to **see**
in the world.

—Mahatma Gandhi

The 15-Minute Miracle™

Revealed

Jacquelyn Aldana ⟩⟨ S.o.L.

(inspired by Ron Aldana)

♥ Inner Wisdom Publications

Los Gatos, California

Published by: ♥ Inner Wisdom Publications

PO Box 1341, Los Gatos, CA 95031-1341, USA

(408) 353-2050 →← Fax (408) 353-4663

Website: http://www.15MinuteMiracle.com

North Star logo by Kat Thomas
Photographs by Jodi Taylor-Amark
Artwork for book cover by LaVon Coffin
Computer graphics by ArtToday and Coral Gallery
Inspiration and unconditional love provided by Ron Aldana
Brilliantly edited by Cheri Sunshine Carroll and **SET** (the Supreme Editing Team)

Copyright © 2003
First Edition, First Printing 1995
First Edition, Second Printing, 1998
First Edition, Third Printing, 2001
Completely Revised Second Edition, First Printing 2002
Completely Revised Second Edition, Second Printing, 2003

Library of Congress Catalog Card Number 2002105333

Publisher's - Cataloging In Publication
(Provided by Quality Books, Inc.)

Aldana, Jacquelyn, 1943
     The 15-Minute Miracle revealed / by Jacquelyn Aldana.

     -- 2nd ed.
     p. cm
     Fifteen-Minute Miracle revealed
     Fifteen Minute Miracle revealed
     Includes bibliographical references and index.
     LCCN 2002105333
     ISBN 0-9656741-9-3

     1. Self-actualization (Psychology) 2. Inspiration.
     3. Self-help techniques.   I. Title. II. Title:
     Fifteen-Minute Miracle revealed III. Title: Fifteen
     Minute Miracle revealed

BF637.S4.A53 2002   158.1

                    QB133-516

Printed in the United States of America

7 6 5 4 3 2 - 07 06 05 04

If you are unable to order this book from your local bookseller, you may order directly from the publisher by calling **1-(888) In The Flow** (that's 1-888-468-4335).

This "feel-good" book was
l♥vingly written for all those
who have a sincere desire to transform

Fear *into* *L♥ve,*

Worry *into* *Well-Being,*
&
Scarcity *into* *Abundance.*

May each and every person who reads
it experience a comforting sense
of "coming home."

Special ✴ Dedication

This book may never have been written had it not been for my loving husband Ron. He has truly been my DEAREST FRIEND for nearly 30 years. We met in 1973 and were married less than a year later. He faithfully promised if I would marry him that he would delight in providing whatever my heart desired for the rest of my life, and he certainly has lived up to his promise.

When I asked him why he wanted to spend the rest of his life with ME, he gently took both of my hands in his and gazed at me softly. He smiled warmly and said with an impish twinkle in his eye, "Although I love you just the way you ARE, I look forward to witnessing the ENORMOUS POTENTIAL I see within you." In that moment I had no idea what he was referring to, but he certainly made me feel SPECIAL.

After 20 years of waiting for my potential to emerge, Ron's unshakable faith in me was finally rewarded in ways that truly surprised BOTH of us. In November of 1991, when he was told he had little hope of survival due to a virulent cancer, I became absolutely DETERMINED to find some way to help him regain his wellness. After exhausting all known possibilities, there was nothing left for us to do but to **surrender and pray** — SURRENDER our FEARS and PRAY for a MIRACLE! That's when we realized that all things really ARE possible when we make the steadfast COMMITMENT to find SOLUTIONS. Although this near-fatal episode certainly challenged us both, it turned out to be the necessary catalyst that relentlessly drove me to discover what we now endearingly refer to as The 15-Minute ✴ Miracle™.

It is because of my loving partner that so many others who are actively looking for answers may be able to find them. Because of Ron, I was divinely inspired to write this book and share a message that has the potential to make a positive difference in countless lives. Of course, I always KNEW that my husband was very SPECIAL, and now I clearly know WHY.

Table of Contents

⫻ Acknowledgments

I wish to acknowledge all the wise and wonderful teachers who came before me to show me the way. I particularly want to thank my favorite inspiring role model Napoleon Hill, who sparked my awareness of human potential way back in 1969. I also wish to express my heartfelt appreciation to Oprah Winfrey, Marlo Morgan, Louise Hay, Wayne Dyer, Dr. Deepak Chopra, Jose Silva, Marianne Williamson, Neale Donald Walsch, Jack Canfield, and Mark Victor Hansen for their positive influence as well. I am especially grateful to Jerry and Esther Hicks, who made it easy for me to focus upon the path of unlimited positive possibilities through their inspiring audiotapes. All of you were "the wind beneath my wings" as I was learning to fly. Thank you for being the SHINING LIGHTS that made such a pleasant and empowering difference in my life.

As I eagerly searched for a greater understanding of Life, I was guided to read several inspiring BOOKS and was drawn to listen to many thought-provoking AUDIOTAPES. The ones that uplifted and inspired me the most are listed in the bibliography as:

Inspirational Food for Thought

Most of all, I wish to offer my warmest and sincerest thanks to You, God, for You are the LOVING POWER in my life who gently guided and supported me every step of the way. I so appreciate Your comforting presence and infinite patience. Please continue to remind me that we are ALL divine expressions of Your unconditional love. I am so grateful that You blessed all mankind with the FREEDOM to follow their dreams, and I am especially glad that You gave each of us the fertile seeds of omnificent potential to joyfully SING the SONG that we came here to SING.

Jacquelyn Aldana ⫻ S.o.L.
Student Of Life ⫻ Seeker Of Light
Sender Of Love ⫻ So Obviously Lucky

My Magnificent ✳ Miracle Team

If this book touches your heart and makes a positive difference in your life, please give credit to the remarkable people below who provided the love, support, and resources that enabled me to write it. I wish to express my heartfelt appreciation to...

- **Ron Aldana** for being my husband, my best friend, and my most avid supporter.
- **Heathcliff Aldana** for his loving heart, playful demeanor, and extraordinary insights.
- **Ronnie Aldana** for his incredibly valuable feedback and perpetual encouragement.
- **Kim Browning** for her loving support, intelligent comments, and super suggestions.
- **Jonathan Bachelor** for being the most loving and caring "big brother" on the planet.
- **Michael Bisbiglia** for helping us to make our Miracle Playshops the best they can be.
- **Debba Boles** for showing us how to dispel darkness by choosing to radiate light.
- **Gayle Bradshaw** for reminding me to keep "The Miracle Message" purely positive.
- **Trace and Debi Butkovich** for training my computer to be more "author friendly."
- **Marymae Cioffi** for her willingness to do whatever was needed to make my life easier.
- **LaVon Coffin** for the incredibly beautiful book cover that she created for this book.
- **Stephanie Coffin** for proving it is truly possible to transcend an "incurable" dis-ease.
- **Country Girl** for doing her part by staying up late each night to keep me company.
- **John and Elinor Crittenden** for giving me the ultimate gift — the "Gift of Life."
- **Cheri Ellison** for helping me to make The Miracle Process the best it has ever been.
- **God** for allowing me to be the one to write His book and to share His message.
- **Isabel Hewett** for inviting us to share our "Miracle Message" with Barnes &Noble.
- **Sunnee Kee-Roman** for her encouragement and her unshakable belief in this work.
- **Gracie Laake** for giving me the gift of several 3-hour massages. My body is so grateful.
- **Al Loukinen** for being the only dad I ever knew. I am all that I am because of him.
- **Elsie (Duffie) Loukinen** for taking me in to raise me as her very own. Thanks, Mom.
- **Pamela Masters** for pouring forth her endless inspiration, love, and magnificent self.
- **Harold and Gladys McCoy** for endorsing this work and inviting me to speak at ORI.
- **Yana Mocak** and **Jennifer Staver** for their exceptional proofreading and editing talents.
- **Brooke Peterson** for being such a persistent pioneer in the world of human potential.
- **Dan Poynter** for teaching me the most valuable things to know about self-publishing.
- **Gillian Sands** for asking questions that caused me to summon greater understanding.
- **Jodi Taylor-Amark** for her loyalty, integrity, and remarkable ability to do everything.
- **Leigh Wunce** for giving me the homework that led to the discovery of this process.
- **Each and every person** who (in any way) contributed to the creation of this book.

Foreword

by Harold McCoy

As Founder and Director of **ORI** (the **O**zark **R**esearch **I**nstitute), I have had the pleasure of connecting with many talented authors and speakers who have created unique and proven ways to empower people to demonstrate their highest potential. At ORI, our primary mission is to make it easy for our 2,300 members to discover practical and productive ways to harness the **power of thought**. This is why our board continues to invite Jacquelyn Aldana to come to our headquarters in Fayetteville, Arkansas, time after time to share her empowering 15-Minute ✳ Miracle message. People love to hear how she and her husband Ron "triumphed over tragedy" in ways that were truly miraculous! Her story gives them hope that they too can attract and create miracles in their own lives.

When I first met Jacquelyn in 1994, she was wrestling with the three greatest challenges of her entire life. Her husband Ron was dying of cancer, their marriage was falling apart at the seams, and their business was nearly bankrupt. Several months later, I was astounded to hear that Ron had completely regained his wellness, their relationship was better than ever, and their business was absolutely thriving! This peaked my curiosity, so I called to find out how all this came about. Jacquelyn said that she had stumbled upon something amazingly simple that seemed to attract miracles into their lives on a consistent basis. She was sure she had found "the missing piece to the puzzle of Life." Because her methodology took only 15 minutes a day to do and consistently yielded miraculous results, she appropriately referred to her fascinating discovery as The 15-Minute ✳ Miracle™.

What began as Jacquelyn and Ron's "personal survival tool" soon became a wonderful "tool for transformation" for those who were desperately searching for answers to such perplexing questions as: 1) "Why isn't my life working?" 2) "What can I do when I really feel stuck?" 3) "How can I find the kind of joy and personal fulfillment that lasts?" You will be glad to know that the answers to these and many more frequently asked questions are all thoroughly explained in **The 15-Minute Miracle™ Revealed** — an easy-to-read book that is filled with ageless wisdom that will cause you to want to read it again and again.

Jacquelyn wrote this book with the intention of clearly revealing how most anyone can rise above prevailing circumstances to enjoy a higher quality of life. She and Ron believe this discovery was divinely inspired and consider it to be a magnificent gift for all to enjoy. Because the principles are based upon universal laws, The 15-Minute ✦ Miracle seems to transcend things like age, gender, status, culture, walk of life, and religious belief systems. It even works well for those who are skeptical about things that seem "too good to be true."

This book can't help but offer you extraordinary hope and encouragement no matter what challenges you may be facing at this time. It shows you how to enrich your state of being by learning to work in harmony with the basic universal laws that govern the quality of your life. What Jacquelyn discovered along her enlightening journey is what YOU can expect to experience for yourself as you read this thought-provoking book. In her humorous and articulate way, she clearly explains how most anyone can enhance their life and attract extraordinary blessings by simply employing a few easy-to-use principles.

Once you see how consistently The 15-Minute ✦ Miracle really works, you will be eager to share it with those near and dear to you. We at ORI are convinced that this empowering book has the potential to uplift the consciousness of the entire planet! Find out how you can harness the elements of serendipity and synchronicity to become the "master of your own destiny." Discover how you can experience a more fulfilling life by setting aside just 15 minutes a day to invite your **desires to be realized** and your **dreams to come true**.

Harold McCoy, Founder and Director
Ozark Research Institute — Fayetteville, Arkansas
www.OzarkResearch.org

Disclaimer

What you are about

to read may cause you

to experience an extraordinary

sense of comfort, self-empowerment,

and inexplicable joy. This book tends to be

physically, mentally, emotionally, and spiritually

addictive. The positive effects are extremely **contagious**

and may cause epidemic proportions of positive possibilities

with all those who come in direct contact with it. Should you

experience an overabundance of ✴ Miracles while applying

the simple principles, please set this book aside until

the euphoria subsides.

Warning

Under no circumstances should anyone ever indulge in
The 15-Minute ✴ Miracle for more than 24 hours a day!

Please Read at Your Own Risk!

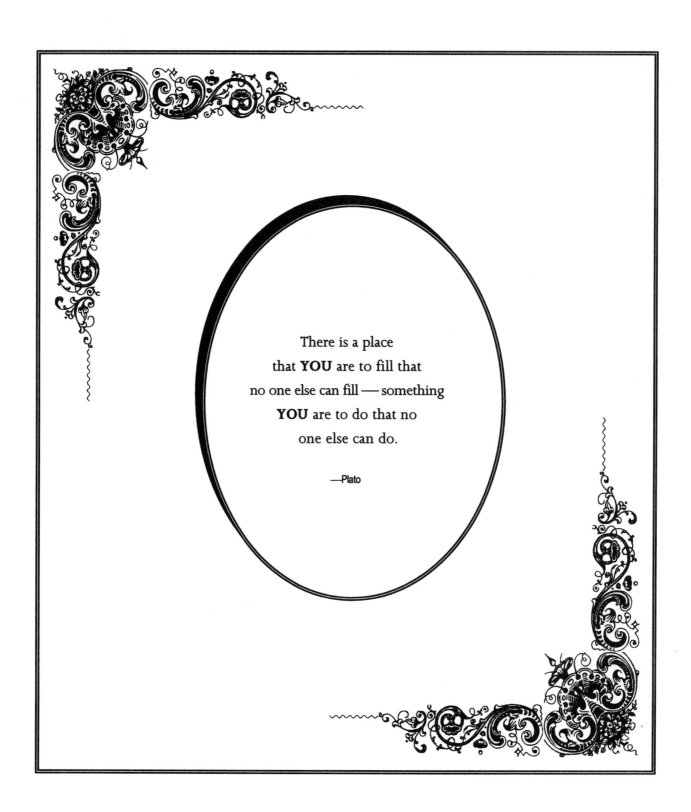

There is a place
that **YOU** are to fill that
no one else can fill — something
YOU are to do that no
one else can do.

—Plato

Part 1

Irresistible

...that which is
absolutely **impossible**
to successfully resist.

How to Become an
"Irresistible ⟶✦⟵ Magnet for Miracles"

Magnetizing miracles into your life is much EASIER than you might think. I feel qualified to say this, because I became an "Irresistible Magnet for Miracles" at a time in my life when my whole world was UPSIDE DOWN. It was BECAUSE of the challenges that I discovered an incredibly simple way to raise my energy and get into "the flow of Life." It was BECAUSE my husband was dying of cancer, BECAUSE our 20-year marriage was "on the rocks," and BECAUSE we were nearly bankrupt that I finally SURRENDERED and asked for HELP! It all started one day when I shouted right out loud to Life,

"Either show me a way to experience more **joy**
in my life or just come and take me **right now!**"

In other words, I wanted Life to either **show me a way** or **haul me away**, and I had absolutely NO ATTACHMENT to the outcome! Just moments later, I was inspired to write something down on a piece of paper that ultimately resulted in my husband completely regaining his WELLNESS, our relationship becoming a "marriage made in HEAVEN," and our business getting back on its feet almost OVERNIGHT! What I wrote down that day turned out to be the forerunner of the magical process we now call 𝕿𝖍𝖊 15-Minute ✦ Miracle. Listed below are the FIVE most important things for you to know in order to become IRRESISTIBLE when it comes to attracting MIRACLES into your life:

1. CLARIFY your dreams and desires by WRITING them down.

2. APPRECIATE what you ALREADY HAVE before asking for MORE.

3. THINK ABOUT, TALK ABOUT, and ENVISION only what you DO WANT.

4. NOTICE how you FEEL in every moment (feelings of comfort or discomfort).

5. Make it your ONGOING INTENTION to be "The HAPPIEST Person You Know."

Expect ✳ Miracles Every Day

Three years prior to discovering 𝕮𝖍𝖊 15-Minute ✳ Miracle, my life was like watching reruns of a bad movie on a TV with poor reception. Just about the time when I thought things couldn't possibly get any worse, THEY DID! When I stumbled onto a simple way to manifest MIRACLES into my life through the power of THOUGHT and PRAYER, I was sure I had found Aladdin's Lamp. As I spent just 15 minutes each day simply writing a LOVE LETTER to LIFE, everything began to fall into place for me EASILY, EFFORTLESSLY, MIRACULOUSLY and MAGICALLY! It wasn't until much later that I realized that all of the amazing manifestations that surprisingly showed up were merely BYPRODUCTS of seeking "sustained joy." As I made it my ongoing intention to find ways to become "The Happiest Person I Knew," everything else took care of itself with LITTLE or NO EFFORT on my part.

Although this intriguing process often results in manifesting desirable circumstances and wonderful MATERIAL things, the REAL VALUE of 𝕮𝖍𝖊 15-Minute ✳ Miracle is that it creates a DIVINE CONNECTION between YOU and your HIGHER POWER, YOU and your MAGNIFICENCE, and YOU and LIFE (in other words, YOU and YOU)! When this happens, things begin to align PERFECTLY and fall into place EASILY. This is probably why so many people associate what they begin to experience with MIRACLES. The best part is that miracles can happen to YOU (when, that is, you are ready and willing to experience them).

Allow us to save you a lot of time and energy that you might otherwise spend pushing, pulling, struggling, swimming upstream, running uphill, and trying to control the outcome of circumstances. Simply SURRENDER your worries, doubts, and fears to your Higher Power and TRUST that Life will reveal Its grandest plan to you in just the perfect time. The difference between trusting and controlling is this: TRUSTING is equivalent to hiring a TEAM of experts to get the job done, whereas CONTROLLING is equal to trying to do all of the work YOURSELF. Until I let go of my need to CONTROL EVERYTHING in my life, EVERYTHING in my life continued to CONTROL ME! I finally had to resign as "CEO of the Universe" in order to transform my stress into peace of mind. We hope the success stories on the following pages will inspire, uplift, and encourage YOU to do the same.

14

Amazing ✦ Miracles

that **Touch the Heart** and **Tickle the Soul**

Looking for Joy in All the Wrong Places

by Cheri Ellison ⊁← S.o.L. (Student of Life) of Palo Alto, California

Before discovering 𝕿𝖍𝖊 15-𝕸𝖎𝖓𝖚𝖙𝖊 ⊁← 𝕸𝖎𝖗𝖆𝖈𝖑𝖊, my life felt like one big "do-over." I had professional counseling for 30 years and spent over $100,000 on self-help seminars and classes. I even walked on fire, meditated, prayed till my knees were sore, and often went to church three times on Sunday! When this failed to bring much fulfillment, I did rebirthing work, soul retrieval, and went to Native American sweat lodges. When still nothing changed for the better, I took public speaking classes and filled my entire home (including my kitchen cabinets) with self-help books, tapes, and videos. After a while, I was feeling so hopeless, helpless, and frustrated that I even participated in a process that required me to jump from the top of a telephone pole to catch a trapeze-like device. This was supposed to build my confidence and courage, but all it really did was make me realize that I had been "chasing the wind" for three decades. I felt totally abandoned by God and I was not the least bit happy about much of anything!

It wasn't until I became aware of 𝕿𝖍𝖊 15-𝕸𝖎𝖓𝖚𝖙𝖊 ⊁← 𝕸𝖎𝖗𝖆𝖈𝖑𝖊 that I even dared to hope that my life had much promise or purpose. Suddenly, I just knew that I had finally found what I had been searching for all of my adult life. After attending the weekend Playshop, my entire life (as Jacquelyn says) began to turn around "at the speed of thought." For the first time in decades, I felt totally content, peaceful, and grateful to be alive. My self-confidence and well-being soared right off the charts. God and I were back on speaking terms — in fact, we had become best friends. My 15-year history of severe acne-rosacia and my morbid fear of death and flying completely disappeared. My business reached levels of productivity that set all-time records. My energy level and enthusiasm became extremely high as a result of finally mustering up the courage to speak my truth right from my heart. This liberated my spirit beyond words. As a result of sharing this message with others, I was blessed to meet "the man of my dreams" who turned out to be "the Love of my life." Because I made a clear commitment to completely master 𝕿𝖍𝖊 15-𝕸𝖎𝖓𝖚𝖙𝖊 ⊁← 𝕸𝖎𝖗𝖆𝖈𝖑𝖊, Jacquelyn allowed me to act as her personal assistant, which was another dream-come-true for me. Thanks to this incredible process, my life is a series of miracles, one right after the other. My entire family and our leadership team from work have been through the Level I Playshop and many of them could write an entire book about their remarkable miracles!

Finding My Way Back Home

by Brent Carroll ⚜ S.o.L. of Fayetteville, Arkansas

If just two months ago someone were to tell me that I would fall in love with Life, with God, with myself, and with that "special someone" I have waited for all of my life, I would have said they were absolutely crazy or (at the very least) misinformed. Well, I am here to tell you that all of this is exactly what happened as a result of discovering a remarkable process called *The 15-Minute* ⚜ *Miracle*. It all started when I was chosen to videotape Jacquelyn Aldana's Miracle ⚜ Mastery Playshop at the Ozark Research Institute in February of 2002. Unlike the other 50 presentations that I had videotaped over the years, this one spoke to me at the very depths of my soul. As I listened to the heartfelt testimonial of Jacquelyn's assistant, Cheri Ellison, I realized that there was someone else who, just like me, had experienced enormous despair. The best part is that she had found a way to reconnect with Life and had found a sense of fulfillment that most people only dare to dream about. I too longed to find the same degree of joy that Cheri had so enthusiastically talked about.

The following day, when I attended the Playshop as a participant, I found it very difficult to connect with my feelings — it was way too painful to allow myself to feel much of anything. All I experienced was the same despair, darkness, and utter lack of hope that I had felt since the day I was born. I honestly felt as though I were in a dark room with no direction and with nothing to connect with that gave me any sense of hope. I often lamented over two failed marriages and the loss of a job I really enjoyed that had afforded me a lucrative income. I prayed each night that I would never wake up, and each morning when I did awake, I cursed Life for making me face one more hopeless day. Thanks to the infinite patience of Jacquelyn and her friend Cheri, I finally succeeded! By practicing the simple principles of *The 15-Minute* ⚜ *Miracle*, I found a "Highway to Heaven," a "Lifeline to Hope," and a "Roadmap to Joy." I now perceive Life as so very wonderful and precious. I also realize that my challenges were all part of God's divine plan to bring me to the glorious place where I am now. As I do my 15-Minute ⚜ Miracle each day, I honestly feel as though I am writing a "love letter to Life" then giving it to God to deliver it as He sees fit in His infinite wisdom. Now, when I open my eyes each morning, the first thing I do is give thanks to God, Cheri Ellison, Jacquelyn Aldana and *The 15-Minute* ⚜ *Miracle*!

17

Miracle Solution for MS
by Stephanie Coffin ✳ S.o.L. of Salinas, California

When I was officially diagnosed with MS in 1994, my life, as I knew it, was over. Not only was I devoid of energy, but I also suffered with severe pain, spasms, and insomnia. To make things even worse, my driver's license was revoked because I was subject to seizures. I was really scared when my doctors predicted that my condition would become progressively worse. While visiting my older sister in Hawaii, I had a chance to read the original manuscript of **The 15-Minute ✳ Miracle™ Revealed** that she was in the process of proofreading. As soon as I began to experiment with it, I noticed an incredible difference. For the first time in over a year, I could get through an entire day without several naps. I began to sleep well at night and the pain and spasms in my body began to quickly subside. Because I had no more seizures, I was also able to get my driver's license reinstated. After faithfully practicing my 15-Minute ✳ Miracle twice a day for only three weeks, I no longer had one symptom of MS!

When I miss a day of doing this process, I pay for it dearly. I don't even get out of bed in the morning until I create my positive intentions for the day. This way, everything I do seems easy, my body remains comfortable, and my energy level stays high. I actually feel better now than I ever have in my entire life. I cannot even imagine going through the rest of my life without The 15-Minute ✳ Miracle. Thanks so much for giving me my life back!

A Lot of Gain with No Pain
by Janette Walton of Yuma, Arizona

Just shortly before I discovered The 15-Minute ✳ Miracle, I was in such physical pain and financial distress that I sometimes felt like giving up — it seemed as though things would never get better. I was unable to find a decent job, and the arthritis in my knees was almost unbearable. Being "positive minded" was very difficult for me at first. I was so busy dwelling on everything that bothered me, that finding the good in anything seemed impossible. Once I started to focus on what I really appreciated in my life, however, I began to feel a little bit better. After doing the process for about three days, I noticed that I my energy was higher, my body felt more flexible, and my attitude was more positive. The improvement in my health was absolutely astounding! I am glad to report that I am now doing better than I ever have in my entire life. I enjoy more comfort in my body and I truly see the beauty in everything. I even started my own business and I am making a lot more money and having much more fun than I ever did working for someone else. I am so glad I found 𝕿𝖍𝖊 15-𝓜𝖎𝖓𝖚𝖙𝖊 ⭢⭠ 𝓜𝖎𝖗𝖆𝖈𝖑𝖊. Every day is now filled with exciting opportunities and wonderful surprises. I actually wonder how I ever got along without it!

What About Bob?

by Bob Middleton ⭢⭠ S.o.L. of Escondido, California

My life improved dramatically after attending the 2-day Miracle ⭢⭠ Mastery Playshop. At that time, I was homeless, jobless, and extremely discouraged. Even worse, I had the social stigma of being on parole for three years. I felt totally alone in life — even my wife and family had left me. After I began doing my 15-𝓜𝖎𝖓𝖚𝖙𝖊 ⭢⭠ 𝓜𝖎𝖗𝖆𝖈𝖑𝖊, I was able to sleep at night without the horrible nightmares that had plagued me for decades (flashbacks of the Viet Nam War). I also noticed how much better I felt about myself and about Life in general. I felt so encouraged that I began to share this process with others on parole during my weekly group meetings. Both my doctor (who facilitated the meetings) and my parole officer were so impressed with my improved attitude that I was officially pardoned of most of my parole! Not only that, I now have a good job, I live with people who love me, and my life seems worth living again. It feels so good to have a sense of purpose and belonging.

I now see that the way I think has everything to do with the way my life turns out. I really believe that everyone in prison and in parole programs should know about this process. In fact, I now volunteer my time to teach it to those who want to learn how to make it work in their own lives. I often wonder how my life might have been had I learned about things like this as a child. If I knew then what I know now, I seriously doubt that I would have ever ended up in prison. Who knows, perhaps someday I can share it with someone who has enough influence to get it into the public school system. It sure feels good to do something that makes other people feel better about themselves. Every time I say something that offers another person just a little bit of hope, I reassure myself that Life can get better for me as well. By the way, if anyone dares to tell you that miracles don't happen and that dreams never come true, you can be absolutely sure that they haven't heard about 𝕿𝖍𝖊 15-𝓜𝖎𝖓𝖚𝖙𝖊 ⭢⭠ 𝓜𝖎𝖗𝖆𝖈𝖑𝖊!

Have Miracle—Will Travel!

by Debbie Voltura of San Francisco, California

For the past two years, I have struggled to find work that offered me a sense of well-being and personal fulfillment. One day a close friend of mine suggested that I casually experiment with 𝕮𝖍𝖊 15-𝕸𝖎𝖓𝖚𝖙𝖊 ⇥ 𝕸𝖎𝖗𝖆𝖈𝖑𝖊. It was really amazing! I felt better immediately after filling in the blanks on the simple form! I wrote that I wanted to receive an extraordinary opportunity to express my full potential as a professional singer in a way that would ignite my passion for living. I specifically requested that it be fun and exciting, as well as financially rewarding. I also asked that it be revealed to me ASAP.

Less than 90 minutes later the phone rang. Adrenaline flooded my veins when I realized who was calling! It was the highly acclaimed author and speaker, Louise L. Hay! She personally invited me to tour with her for the purpose of providing musical inspiration for her series of *Empowering Women Seminars*. Wow! What a perfect opportunity to become abundantly prosperous while doing what I love more than anything else in the world — freely expressing my feelings through my music. If 𝕮𝖍𝖊 15-𝕸𝖎𝖓𝖚𝖙𝖊 ⇥ 𝕸𝖎𝖗𝖆𝖈𝖑𝖊 had anything to do with this synchronistic event, I can hardly wait to do it again!

Putting 𝕮𝖍𝖊 15-𝕸𝖎𝖓𝖚𝖙𝖊 ⇥ 𝕸𝖎𝖗𝖆𝖈𝖑𝖊 to the Test

by Debbie Voltura of San Francisco, California

I had already experienced incredible results only 90 minutes after doing my first 15-𝕸𝖎𝖓𝖚𝖙𝖊 ⇥ 𝕸𝖎𝖗𝖆𝖈𝖑𝖊. Just in case it was only a fluke, however, I decided to really put this enigmatic process to the test. To see what would happen, I playfully requested three things that I felt were "a bit much to ask for." First, I requested a special parking spot right in front of every single place that I intended to go that day (the odds of winning the lottery are higher than finding even one such parking place in San Francisco). Then I vividly imagined receiving some form of unexpected income, plus a delightful surprise gift that would tickle my fancy. Here is an account of what actually happened all in one day:

I magically found a parking spot right in front of the first place I went that day. Although pleased, I wasn't overly impressed. When I found my perfect parking spots at the next four places, however, I became ecstatic! Later, I was dumbfounded when I opened my car door only to find a dollar bill lying in the street (the unexpected income I had playfully imagined)! As if that weren't enough, I picked up the dollar bill and almost passed out from shock — right underneath it was a beautiful 14k-gold bracelet (obviously the surprise gift I had envisioned)! Well, I don't need any further dramatic demonstrations to prove that The 15-Minute Miracle actually works. I now look forward to each new day, because this "Game of Life" has just become much more fun to play!

From Wishes to Realities
by Brooke Peterson S.o.L. of Loxahatchee, FL

For the first time in my life, I feel as though I have the power to attract and create a desirable quality of life for myself. Before I became aware of The 15-Minute Miracle, I often felt very confused and frustrated. I constantly struggled trying to find ways to make things happen. Now I enjoy total clarity and a definite sense of purpose in my life. Whenever I get stuck, I simply turn to my 15-Minute Miracle process and it works every time!

Within just three days of experimenting with this process for the first time, I manifested the perfect job that paid me abundantly and provided the flexibility I needed to pursue my dreams. Shortly after that, I reestablished my own executive placement business. Since I began sending all of my employees to the Playshops and providing my clients with Miracle Starter Kits, my personal and professional achievements have just skyrocketed! I was able to manifest over $300,000 in less than a year working only part time out of my home.

I used to think I didn't have time to squeeze one more process into my busy day, but the more time I invest in my 15-Minute Miracle, the more success and abundance I seem to experience. I now enjoy incredible health, more love in my life, and I feel on top of the world (even when Life offers challenges from time to time). The best part is that it is all so easy. Each time I meet someone who appears to be overwhelmed and discouraged, I delight in sharing my remarkable "miracle stories." After an entire lifetime of searching for answers and solutions to Life's many mysteries, I am convinced that this is, by far, the best life-enhancement tool available today. It feels so good to be referred to as a "living example of prosperity" and a "loving expression of joy." I plan to do all that I can to share this message with those who are ready and wanting to hear it.

The Awesome Power of Appreciation

by Gemma Bauer ⊁← S.o.L. of Felton, California

For over 10 years, I suffered with the excruciating pain of rheumatoid arthritis. I tried just about every healing modality imaginable, but nothing seemed to bring relief. I read Jacquelyn's book and did the process, but after seeing no results in three days, I decided it was just one more thing that had no benefit. It wasn't until I attended a Playshop that I discovered why it hadn't worked for me. In my eagerness to feel better, I skipped the first step (The Appreciation Step). Little did I realize that a heartfelt expression of gratitude is what opens the door to attracting everything else in The 15-Minute ⊁← Miracle process!

On the morning after the Playshop, I did my 15-Minute ⊁← Miracle with a renewed enthusiasm. This time, I made sure to first write about the many things I appreciated. Next, I elaborated upon how I love to feel flexible and comfortable in my body. In Step #7, I envisioned myself doing something very special that day with my mate, Neal. In that very moment, I felt a wave of comfort and ease flooding my entire body. There was no doubt in my mind that something very wonderful was about to happen!

Just then Neal awoke and suggested we drive up the coast to find a special place to enjoy the day together. As we walked briskly through the deep sand on a picturesque beach, Neal shouted, "Look, Gemma — you're able to jog and you're not even limping!" Only then did I realize how comfortable, flexible, and easy all of my movements were. What an incredible miracle to feel such tremendous freedom in my body. What is even more amazing is that I hadn't even taken my pain medication that day!

My prayers were finally answered and my dreams really did come true. I feel as though my life has just begun. This experience now enables me to know that limitations are in the past. As a result of releasing so much negativity in my life, my body naturally released harmful toxins and the excess weight I had carried for years, which was another fantastic bonus I never would have expected! Your kind words, your loving thoughts, and your extraordinary insights have deeply touched my life. Mere words cannot even begin to convey how very grateful Neal and I are to you, your courageous husband, and the magical 15-Minute ⊁← Miracle. You and Ron have made my life worth living again. May God bless you both and reward you abundantly.

Hope, Faith, and Miracles
by Jeanie Parker ✻ S.o.L. of Los Gatos, California

I will never forget how I felt last year when I found out I was in stage 4 of a serious inoperable lung cancer. I could see by the look on my doctor's face that my prognosis was very poor. After recovering from the initial shock, I became absolutely determined to find a way to live! On our way home from the doctor, my husband and I decided to go see Ron Aldana, because we remembered seeing him when his frail body was limp and lifeless due to his battle with cancer. We were astonished, just a couple of years later, to see him looking totally vital and healthy. When we asked how he managed to overcome his disease, he shared his incredible story about The 15-Minute ✻ Miracle. He was sure that the simple journaling process he did every day was responsible for saving his life! Ron and Jacquelyn spent about three hours talking to us and showing us what to do and how to do it. A few weeks later, we learned even more when we attended a Miracle ✻ Mastery Playshop.

Only eight months after my apparently hopeless diagnosis, my doctors announced that my cancer was in remission. They were absolutely amazed! When I went for another checkup four months later, I was still in remission (and I plan to stay in remission)! I am so grateful each and every day. Although I had six months of chemotherapy, acupuncture, and supplements, I contribute most of my healing to God, The 15-Minute ✻ Miracle, and my special prayer group (consisting of only four people) that met every single week for the purpose of helping me regain my wellness.

From "Down 'N Out" to "Up 'N At 'Em"
by Sunnee Kee-Roman ✻ S.o.L. of Grass Valley, California

When I first met Jacquelyn, I was extremely depressed as a result of a serious illness that had left me unable to work. When my boyfriend became overwhelmed with my problems and decided to leave, I was devastated. Thank God a close friend called and told me about The 15-Minute ✻ Miracle. She said, "If your life is not exactly the way you want it to be, just do this amazing little process and watch the miracles start to magically flow into your life." I called and ordered the books immediately! As soon as they arrived, I began doing the process right away. I specifically asked for three things: 1) to fully regain my health, 2) to attract a loving life partner who wanted to spend the rest of his life with me, and 3) to find a way to make a prosperous living doing something fun. As of this writing, my health is at an all-time high and I can't remember when I have ever been more content. It is hard to even recall how discouraged I felt before, because my life is so extraordinary now. So many opportunities have come my way, that my biggest challenge is in deciding which ones to accept! Best of all, I am "living the life I love" happily married to "the Love of my life." We have our own business making such abundant income that we can afford to make decisions based solely upon our preferences. As far as I'm concerned, The 15-Minute ✳ Miracle is equivalent to oxygen. This is why I definitely plan to use it for the rest of my life!

And Then There Was Light
by Debba Boles ✳ S.o.L. of Grass Valley, California

Prior to becoming aware of The 15-Minute ✳ Miracle, I was clinically depressed and extremely suicidal for well over five years. Since I had a wonderful son who loved and adored me, I knew that "taking my own life" was definitely out of the question. My dilemma, however, was "How was I going to be able to continue to live in this valley of hopeless overwhelm?" Although doctors experimented with over 30 different anti-depressant drugs to treat my symptoms of chronic depression, nothing seemed to help. I tried hypnotherapy, counseling, and just about everything short of electroshock therapy. I felt as though I would always be trapped in darkness and I desperately wanted out!

After reading the 15-Minute ✳ Miracle books that were given to me by my cousins Kathleen and Michelle, I decided to enroll in the next Miracle ✳ Mastery Playshop. What a life-changing experience that was! For the first time in my life, I realized that I deserved to be happy, which allowed me to view life in a completely different way. As soon as I began to focus upon things I truly appreciated, I began to notice a multitude of miracles showing up in my life in ways that often defied logical explanation. In the two years that I have been on this amazing miracle journey, my life has just blossomed into a beautiful state of being. Even when I have my occasional challenging moments, I now know to use my "Miracle Tools," which enable me to quickly regain my balance in ways that feel comfortable. For the five years that I suffered from depression, I was totally unable to work. At this time, however, I am proud to report that I am certified to teach computer classes at various schools and colleges. In fact, Jacquelyn chose me to design and maintain her website and she has also certified me to facilitate Level I Miracle ⇥←Mastery Playshops in Northern California. All is now extremely well in my world and my life has never been better!

I Love My Life
by Linda Adams ⇥← S.o.L. of Monterey, California

Four months ago I was working 50-60 hours a week in a job I didn't like, wondering if I would ever feel joy again. After attending the Level I Miracle ⇥←Mastery Playshop, I quit my job, took a 6-week break then created my perfect job in less than a week after I decided to go back to work. Although I have experienced many wonderful benefits now, the most profound change in my life is that my joy has returned! Last week someone said to me, "You really enjoy your work, don't you?" I realized that I not only enjoy my work, but that I also really enjoy my life. In fact, I love my life now! Each day brings a sense of fulfillment and satisfaction, because I now feel that I can make a positive difference in the lives around me. And the best part is that I can look forward to the rest of my life knowing that miracles and joy will always be a part of it. It is so comforting to know that I now have the tools to get back on track whenever I need to. I am so very grateful for 𝕿𝖍𝖊 15-𝕸𝖎𝖓𝖚𝖙𝖊 ⇥← 𝕸𝖎𝖗𝖆𝖈𝖑𝖊.

From Panic Attacks to Peace of Mind
by Joanne P. Johnson ⇥← S.o.L. of San Jose, California

I had my first panic attack at age 17, and when I was 35, I began to experience them again. I found it very difficult to go anywhere, because I was terrified to leave the house. Until you have experienced the gripping fear that panic attacks evoke, it is hard for the average person to understand what it's like. My worst panic attacks occurred when I began hormone replacement therapy at age 50. I was extremely agoraphobic (afraid of open spaces) and was unable to leave home without my husband or my best friend. I was really discouraged until I saw Jacquelyn Aldana on TV one night. The next day, I called and told her I wanted to attend a Playshop, but that I was afraid to leave the house. She immediately taught me a simple process called The One-Minute ⇥← Miracle, which allowed me to feel safe to leave home, drive my car, and go shopping by myself for the first time in many years. Even when I secretly expected to be plagued by panic attacks from time to time due to challenging circumstances, they didn't seem to erupt. After attending the Level I Miracle ⇥← Mastery Playshop, I felt more confident and courageous than ever. I truly believe that just learning

The One-Minute ⚹ Miracle, 𝕿𝖍𝖊 15-𝕸inute ⚹ 𝕸iracle, and the Universal Language of Life enabled me to enjoy a much higher quality of life. With total confidence, I highly recommend 𝕿𝖍𝖊 15-𝕸inute ⚹ 𝕸iracle materials and Playshops for anyone who suffers from agoraphobia and panic attacks. If they can work miracles for me, I am sure they can work for anyone!

Happy Endings and New Beginnings
by Judy Dotson ⚹ S.o.L. of San Jose, California

When I describe my life as it was before practicing 𝕿𝖍𝖊 15-𝕸inute ⚹ 𝕸iracle, it feels as though I am talking about someone else. For well over five years, I had a terrible fear when it came to driving. Within the first hour of the Level I Miracle Mastery ⚹ Playshop, I completely overcame all of my intense anxiety about this issue. I now actually enjoy driving anywhere with complete confidence. Within just one week of attending the Playshop with my husband Kenny, our frequent arguing was replaced with loving words of kindness and caring. As we made it our ongoing intention to "see each other through the eyes of awe and wonder," we kept falling in love all over again! The best part of all is that my internal dialog has become much more positive, which allows me to see the beauty and benefits of Life *regardless* of conditions. People in both my personal and professional life are constantly asking me to tell them how I am able to be consistently happy in spite of challenging circumstances that arise from time to time. I proudly tell them that I simply indulge in my 15-𝕸inute ⚹ 𝕸iracle on a daily basis. I explain that it automatically sets a positive tone for my day, which makes it easy for me to magically attract multitudes of miracles into my life. I am so grateful for this simple little technique, because it addresses all levels of my being and inspires me to count my blessings in every moment. I plan to continue seeking joy and reaching for the stars each and every day for the rest of my life!

From Hopeless Days to Happy Days
by Lisa Racine ⚹ S.o.L. of Thousand Oaks, California

Life is no fun at all when your kids are unhappy, your spouse is discontented, your finances are scarce, you hate your job, and you're struggling every minute of every day just to keep everything together. This is exactly what my life looked like before my sister Robin gave me a copy of The 15-Minute Miracle™ Revealed. As soon as I began to put the principles

26

to work, everything in my life began to immediately change for the better. I was so encouraged with my results that my husband and I drove over 300 miles to go to a weekend Playshop. This was the beginning of a whole new life, not only for me, but also for my entire family. My husband began to interact with our children in ways that inspired them to demonstrate their potential more than ever before. He also created his own business, which turned out to be the best vocational decision he ever made. He is so good at what he does that he is completely booked for over six months! Because he is so happy and feels more fulfilled, our marriage is so much richer now. In fact, we plan to renew our wedding vows this summer in Las Vegas. Another wonderful thing happened in regards to our prosperity when I wrote in my 15-Minute ⇥⇤ Miracle that I love to receive unexpected income. Shortly thereafter, my accountant called and told me that we are due to receive a refund for over $7,900.00. This definitely exceeded my wildest expectations!

Because of my enormous success with this process, I wanted to share it with others. I recently joined the Miracle Mastery ⇥⇤ Leadership Program and became an official facilitator for the 8-Week Miracle Discovery Program. The majority of my group happened to be members of my family, which provided a wonderful opportunity for all of us to become closer than ever before. I plan to offer another 8-week Miracle Discovery Course in the near future, because it not only benefited my students, but it also added greatly to my own personal growth as well. Whoever would have thought that something so fun and easy could be this powerful? I am so grateful to you, Jacquelyn, for creating this easy-to-do and easy-to-teach program. You and Ron are such blessings in my life. Thank you very much for all that you have done for me and for my entire family.

You TOO Can Make a Positive Difference in the World

If you want to UPLIFT and INSPIRE others, please call us at (408) 353-2050 and share your exciting miracles, or simply fax them to our **Miracle Hotline** at (408) 353-HOME (that's 408-353-4663). You can also go to our website at www.15MinuteMiracle.com and e-mail them to us if that is easier for you. YOUR SUCCESS is OUR SUCCESS and YOUR TESTIMONY can add to the success of many OTHERS. Thank you for taking the time to make such a positive and measurable difference in the lives of those who are seeking solutions!

✳ Shortcut

...a simple way of doing
something more **directly** and
quickly than by ordinary means.
The 15-Minute ✳ Miracle provides an
easy-to-follow **ROADMAP** that clearly
shows many intriguing and time-
saving shortcuts to miracles.

Shortcuts to ✳ Miracles

There is an extremely QUICK and SIMPLE way for you to enjoy a delightfully positive difference in your life. This book tells you HOW you can accomplish this almost immediately REGARDLESS of any challenges you may be experiencing at this time. Get comfortable and give yourself permission to claim the next couple of hours exclusively for YOU. Think of it as taking a well-deserved vacation. Discover how you can have fun consciously creating a richer quality of life for yourself in only **15 minutes a day**. Although many believe that miracles are quite RARE and witnessed by very FEW, we believe that miracles are readily ACCESSIBLE to absolutely ANYONE who is willing and ready to experience them.

Because this book has only 172 pages with plenty of white space, you can probably read it in only a few sittings. We have DELIBERATELY utilized special effects and have mentioned certain things more than once in order to EMPHASIZE the ideas that are most important for you to comprehend. This approach has proven to be very beneficial. It enables you to magically absorb and digest the empowering essence of *The 15-Minute ✳ Miracle* so that you TOO can begin to experience a measurable sense of PERSONAL FULFILLMENT.

Although the wisdom expressed within the pages of this book was certainly divinely inspired, one does not necessarily need to subscribe to organized religion in order to benefit from this philosophy. Each person's religious and spiritual convictions are very PERSONAL, and we respectfully honor ALL paths that lead to TRUTH. We invite you to selectively TAKE what you can use and simply LEAVE the rest. It is our primary intention that you feel GOOD, become truly EXCITED about Life, and thoroughly ENJOY yourself as you read this book.

Before you officially embark upon your 15-Minute ✳ Miracle journey, we want to offer you a handful of precious diamonds, pearls, and gold nuggets: diamonds of KNOWLEDGE, pearls of WISDOM, and gold nuggets of TRUTH. In the next few pages, we are going to reveal our discovery of WHY so many people NEVER find that elusive sense of personal fulfillment no matter how LONG they search or how HARD they try. If you are sick and tired of bumping into WALLS of FRUSTRATION, you will very likely appreciate the DOORS of OPPORTUNITY that are about to open for you as you explore the remainder of this chapter!

Why "Positive Thinking" Just Isn't Enough

Although success certainly begins with POSITIVE THINKING, we must eventually take POSITIVE ACTION in order to bring about POSITIVE RESULTS. The final step to personal fulfillment, however, is achieving a state of POSITIVE BEING. So many of our clients tell us that they used to think of themselves as very positive minded until they began to pay ATTENTION to the way in which they expressed themselves. They were quite shocked to realize that they most often talked in terms of: 1) what they DIDN'T LIKE, 2) what they DIDN'T WANT, and 3) and what they most FEARED. After learning the "Universal Language of Life," (a purely positive language) they soon realized that they had to think and speak more about what they DID WANT, instead of focusing so much upon what they DIDN'T WANT. Once they began to redirect their attention exclusively upon what they PREFERRED to experience, Life suddenly became a game that was much more fun to play. Not only does POSITIVE FOCUS yield much higher dividends, but it also provides a way to accomplish MORE by doing LESS! What could be more IDEAL than that?

Why Affirmations Don't Always Work

Affirmations, although very empowering, often fail to FOOL the subconscious mind into believing something is TRUE when all evidence points to the CONTRARY. Most people require a BRIDGE TO BELIEVABILITY before affirmations provide much benefit. Although the words, **"I am"** and **"it is"** are extremely powerful, they often invite **IC** (your Inner Critic") to have a regular field day at YOUR expense. For instance, if you were overweight and out of shape and you repeated to yourself over and over and over again, "I am my perfect body weight and size," **IC** would probably mutter, "Oh yeah? Have you looked at yourself in the mirror lately? Get real!" If, however, you REPHRASED this statement and said, **"I love it when** I am my perfect body weight and size," **IT** (your Inner Teacher) would likely say, "It is my pleasure to always give you MORE of whatever you love, Magnificent One. Please allow me to show you how to create a fit and trim body in ways that are FUN and EASY." As silly as this may sound, it has proven to offer ENORMOUS BENEFIT to those who practice it. Without changing anything other than prefacing her affirmations with **"I love it when…"** one of our Playshop graduates released over 35 pounds in less than 10 weeks!

Why Journaling Sometimes Backfires

Several of our readers have said, "I have been faithfully journaling for years and, if anything, my life has become even MORE challenging!" There is actually a very LOGICAL reason for this. If you are writing about how BAD everything is, you are unfortunately attracting the very people, places, and things you dread most. The act of WRITING is a wonderful POWER TOOL when you use it to describe what you DESIRE. When, however, you use it to vent your HOSTILITIES, it becomes a self-sabotaging WEAPON that is destined to UNDERMINE your joy. In other words, anything you are FOR empowers you; anything you are AGAINST weakens you. This is why it is ESSENTIAL that you make wise choices when it comes to putting things in writing. Ancient people of the Nile were convinced that WRITING made things REAL. If this is the case, what do you want to make REAL in YOUR life today?

Why Traditional Therapy Isn't Always Effective

Although traditional therapy can be quite valuable, it often invites us to focus upon things that are NOT WORKING, things that DISTRESS us, and things that cause us to re-experience FEAR and PAIN. Since **"Whatever we FOCUS upon with FEELING gets BIGGER,"** focusing too much upon the NEGATIVE ASPECTS of Life cause us to attract the very things we DON'T WANT! If, for instance, we allow an unhappy CHILDHOOD to dominate our thoughts in our ADULTHOOD, we literally ROB ourselves of the joy that Life is so eager for us to have. When we dwell upon "what's going WRONG in our lives," we inadvertently invite many MORE things to go wrong! That's why it is so important for us to understand the MAGNITUDE of the power we possess. When we begin to focus upon our BLESSINGS, we attract MORE blessings. When we redirect our attention to "what is RIGHT with the world," we begin to experience a much HIGHER quality of life. If you are ready to LIVE the life you LOVE and LOVE the life you LIVE, we invite you to appreciate all the goodness of Life that you ALREADY HAVE and then bask in the positive possibilities that are awaiting your discovery. Take only **1%** of your attention to focus upon what you DON'T WANT and **99%** to focus upon what you PREFER instead. Herein lies the KEY to experiencing a more sustainable sense of joy. As it turns out, LOVE, JOY, and LAUGHTER are truly the best therapy, because they make you FEEL GREAT and offer only POSITIVE SIDE EFFECTS!

Why Getting What We Want Doesn't Always Make Us Happy

I used to think, "IF ONLY I could have everything I want, THEN I would be happy." It wasn't until 1995 (when Life brought me EVERYTHING I asked for at the speed of thought) that I realized that this was DEFINITELY not the case! It was like going to my favorite restaurant and ordering everything on the menu and trying to eat it all at one sitting. Although everything was delicious, it was also extremely overwhelming. It was like trying to satisfy my thirst by drinking from a fire hydrant! Even though I received everything I wanted, I often didn't WANT it once I GOT it. That's when I was inspired to make the following request of Life: "Please bring me only that which serves me BEST at this time, in the most appropriate ways that express the highest good for All Life Everywhere. Instead of always GETTING what I WANT, please arrange for me to WANT what I GET." By allowing Life to unveil Its grandest plan this way, I am MUCH HAPPIER and far MORE CONTENT.

Why "What We THINK and SAY" Really Matters

Although there are many languages throughout the world, the one that can enhance our lives the most is the "Universal Language of Life." To master it, we must choose PURELY POSITIVE WORDS as we speak. It is equally important for us to think PURELY POSITIVE THOUGHTS even when engaging in "self-talk" in the privacy of our own minds. This PURELY POSITIVE LANGUAGE is based upon a universal law called the Law of Magnetic Attraction that is at work EVERY second of EVERY day, whether we are aware of it or not. When we understand how to work in HARMONY with this immutable law, Life is much EASIER. When we are ignorant of it, however, Life can be rather CHALLENGING. This law says, "What we THINK ABOUT is what we BRING ABOUT and what we FILL our minds with our lives are FULL of." In other words, whatever we think about, talk about, observe, or even imagine, is the very thing we (knowingly or unknowingly) ATTRACT to ourselves! Furthermore, Life interprets everything we think or say quite LITERALLY, so we must be very AWARE of our language in order to attract what we truly DESIRE. To thoroughly learn this language and to be able to speak and write it fluently, you may want to consider attending the Level I Miracle ⇥⇤ Mastery Playshop. If you prefer to study at home on your OWN, you'll find the Deluxe Miracle Starter Kit to be a great resource (see page 165 for description).

What Do **Happy People** Do?

1. They always see the MAGNIFICENCE in each and every person they meet.

2. They see the BEAUTY and BENEFITS in Life, REGARDLESS of circumstances.

3. They APPRECIATE all that they ALREADY HAVE before asking for anything ELSE.

4. They find something to LOVE and ADMIRE about EVERYTHING and EVERYONE in EVERY moment.

5. They allow themselves to feel ALL of their feelings so they can choose which ones to KEEP and which ones to RELEASE.

6. They view Life through the eyes of AWE and WONDER like a small child who absolutely KNOWS beyond a shadow of a doubt that all things are truly POSSIBLE.

7. They embrace ALL aspects of Life, both positive and negative, because CONTRAST is an extremely VALUABLE TOOL. By simply knowing what they DON'T WANT, they can better identify what they PREFER instead. What could be easier than this?

8. They totally RELEASE and let go of whatever no longer serves them in a positive way: things like resistance, resentment, condemnation of themselves and others, fear, and attachment to outcomes. (When you let go of THEM, they let go of YOU!)

9. They HOLD THE SPACE for themselves and others to regain their balance in just the PERFECT TIME in ways that bless and benefit everyone. This is one of the most LOVING and SUPPORTIVE things we can do for ourselves or anyone else.

10. They love others even when others are LESS than loving toward them. When other people do something that could be considered OFFENSIVE, they just say to themselves, "That's just them not knowing a BETTER way at this time. If they COULD do better they certainly WOULD do better." This is what we call UNCONDITIONAL LOVE at its very best.

If you make it your ONGOING INTENTION to practice these principles,
you may very well become **"The Happiest Person You Know,"**
as well as an **"Irresistible Magnet for Miracles!"**

Steppingstones

The greatest opportunities
(steppingstones) are often created
out of the biggest adversities (stumbling
blocks). Major challenges may cause some
people to **break**, while they inspire
others to **break records**!

From **Stumbling Blocks** to ✳ **Steppingstones**

Does your life ever feel like an UPHILL BATTLE? Do you find yourself pushing through WALLS of RESISTANCE instead of simply opening DOORS of OPPORTUNITY? Does it feel as though you have been running through wet cement as you RUSH to meet the demands of the day? If so, you will be glad to know that…

- You are certainly **not alone**.
- There is a much **easier way** to proceed.
- You can **consciously create** a much higher quality of life.

Just prior to discovering **The 15-Minute ✳ Miracle** and writing this book, I was at an all-time low in my OWN life. My husband Ron was suffering from a virulent CANCER, our 20-year marriage was ON THE ROCKS, and our business was nearly BANKRUPT. It seemed as though we were in a downward spiral whirling in a negative direction at dizzying speeds. Life, as we knew it, was just NOT FUN any more.

In the past, when my life felt overwhelming, I would take time out to WRITE down any QUESTIONS that were on my mind. This enabled me to more easily ORGANIZE my thoughts so I would know the most appropriate ACTION to take. Since this was a technique that had worked well BEFORE, I figured it was worth pursuing. One afternoon (after feeling as though I had run a 26-mile marathon with my feet tied together) I literally COLLAPSED into my desk chair and scribbled out the following question:

"What exactly is my **purpose** for even being here?"

For some reason, I felt inexplicably COMPELLED to write down the curious response that came into my awareness. It was so STRONG that I couldn't possibly ignore it! As though an UNSEEN HAND was gently guiding my pen, I found myself writing the following statement:

"Discover the **Truth** and share it with **others**."

When I read it back, I was absolutely AWESTRUCK! It seemed so PROFOUND, yet I honestly didn't understand it. "WHAT TRUTH?" I wondered. "WHAT OTHERS?" I pondered. The MORE I thought about it, the MORE I became convinced that I was just losing my grip on reality. Out of the frustration of it all, I simply returned to my private world of struggling to get through just o-n-e m-o-r-e arduous day.

I was SURE that I had dismissed this issue, yet everything I picked up to read seemed to have the word TRUTH leaping off the page. The Truth I am referring to was no ordinary truth, mind you, but rather the BIG Truth — the Truth about LIFE. It was uncanny how many times this word came up in everyday conversations. I began to wonder if it had suddenly become the universal word of choice. Six days after asking God to clarify my life's purpose, I came across the same yellow legal pad I had used to write down my question. When I reread those insightful words, **"Discover the TRUTH and share it with others."** my body became flooded with thrill bumps. W-o-w! I FINALLY realized that this message was NOT to be taken lightly! It was only days later that I discovered the essence of what we now call 𝕿𝔥𝔢 15-Minute ⇥⇤ Miracle. What happened only a short time later is truly a remarkable story.

For openers, my failing relationship with Ron was completely healed only 12 HOURS after applying the simple 15-Minute ⇥⇤ Miracle principles. Within only a few days, our business began to generate more revenue than we had seen in over 20 YEARS. Shortly after Ron began to experiment with this remarkable technique, his health improved dramatically and today he is totally **happy**, **healthy**, and **cancer free**!

Out of my unwavering COMMITMENT and DETERMINATION to find viable solutions, I honestly believe that I was DIVINELY GUIDED to discover this magical process. The results of this profound awareness have been nothing short of MIRACULOUS. When we began to share it with our friends and family, we noticed that they TOO experienced incredible results. After a while, so many people were faxing, e-mailing, calling on the phone, or coming to the door for information that Ron and I had to offer organized gatherings to accommodate all of them — thus The Miracle ⇥⇤ Mastery Playshops were born. It is now our greatest pleasure to reveal our secrets of success in ways that enable ORDINARY people to experience EXTRAORDINARY results.

The 15-Minute ✳ Miracle
literally took on a life of its own!

Shortly after the manuscript of this book had been reviewed by several friends and relatives, we began receiving advance orders from all over the US and Canada. Because we had done absolutely NOTHING in the way of advertising or promotion, we were absolutely amazed that so many people had heard about it just by WORD of MOUTH. Several psychiatrists, psychologists, and marriage and family counselors began to order books for their clients and patients, while others just wanted them as gifts for themselves or their loved ones.

Today, Ron and I feel so blessed to be able to share this empowering message with those who desire to hear it. At first you may think this book is all about us, but as it turns out, Magnificent One, **it's really all about YOU!** It reveals how YOU can consciously design and attract the life of your dreams with amazing ease. There really IS an easier and more enjoyable way to play this wondrous game of Life and we are eager to provide the simple tools that make it EASY for you to enjoy the following:

Good Health ✳ **Abundant Energy** ✳ **Unexpected Income**
Loving Relationships ✳ **A Sense of Well-Being** ✳ **Delightful Surprises**

If you are seeking practical and enjoyable ways to easily CONNECT with your sense of well-being, we think you will be THRILLED with the incredibly simple yet powerful journaling process called **The 15-Minute ✳ Miracle**. In fact, we are quite CONFIDENT that you will enjoy it!

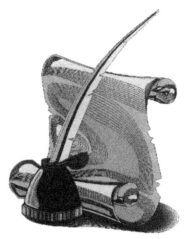

Laughter is the
shortest distance
between two people.

—Victor Borge

Part 2

♥ How Every Day Can Be a Great Day

♥ Frequently Asked Questions

Good news:
What you **want**
wants **you**!

—Debra Jones

How Every Day Can Be a Great Day

Have you ever had one of those EXTRAORDINARY days that made you wish it would never end? You know, one of those days when everything just MAGICALLY fell into place no matter WHAT you did or HOW you did it? Wouldn't it be wonderful if only there were a way to experience days like these more OFTEN? Just imagine how glorious that would be. What usually happens, however, is that we go through our lives thinking we have no control over such things — that some days are just BETTER than others. Right? **WRONG!**

You'll be glad to know that YOU have the power to call these miraculous days into being as often as you choose. This book promises to show you how to create remarkable days, one right after the other. In fact, you will be able to do "these and even GREATER things" by merely applying a few simple principles. All you have to do is understand how certain universal laws operate so you can enjoy the benefits of working in HARMONY with them. Yes, we know, this all sounds TOO GOOD to be TRUE, so please don't take OUR word for it. Just follow the instructions in this book and see what happens. Don't be too surprised, however, when people begin to ask why you are HAPPIER, more ENERGETIC, and more PRODUCTIVE than usual. Next, they will want to know how THEY can accomplish these things!

The next few pages will give you a better idea of what The 15-Minute Miracle is all about. We invite you to discover how you can DELIBERATELY ATTRACT and CONSCIOUSLY CREATE a desirable quality of Life on a CONSISTENT BASIS. Learn how EVERY day can be a wonderful day and how you can easily experience your highest purpose for being. Prepare for an adventure that will very likely inspire you to view Life through the eyes of AWE and WONDER. Get ready to **fall in love** — in love with Life and everything in it (INCLUDING YOURSELF). Life absolutely adores you and is eager to respond to your every desire. All you have to do is figure out what truly makes you HAPPY — the rest is relatively EASY. Life wants you to thoroughly ENJOY your experience here on earth, because…

YOU are the **Divine Creation** in whom your **Creator** is well pleased!

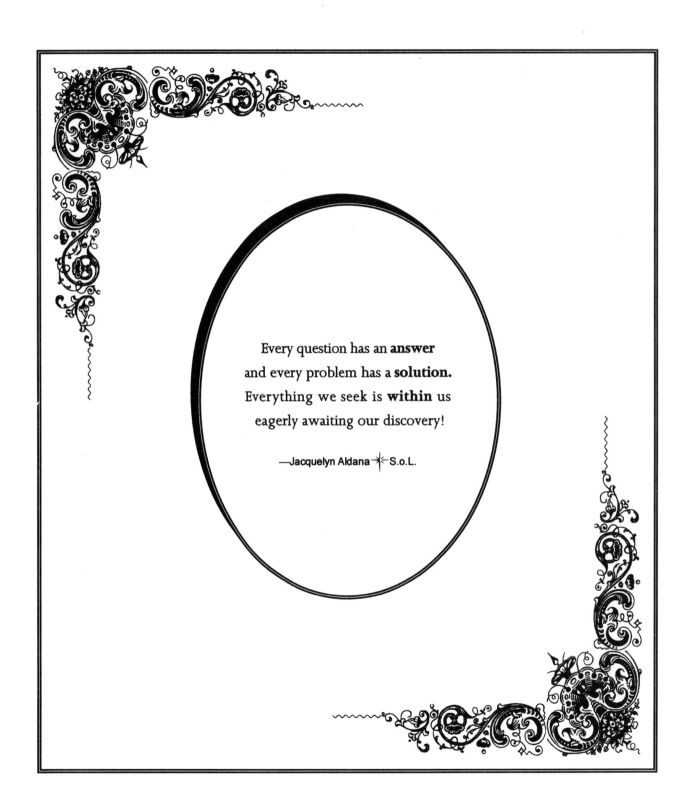

Every question has an **answer**
and every problem has a **solution.**
Everything we seek is **within** us
eagerly awaiting our discovery!

—Jacquelyn Aldana ✳ S.o.L.

Frequently Asked *←* Questions

1. **What exactly is The 15-Minute *←* Miracle?**

   It's an extremely easy-to-do process that leads to incredible feelings of sustained joy, contentment, and inner peace (qualities of absolute bliss). Some refer to it as a "Love Letter to Life," while others think of it as a simple prayer that leads to becoming "The Happiest Person They Know." This user-friendly technique is affectionately referred to as The 15-Minute *←* Miracle, because...

   - It takes only **15 minutes** a day to do (less than 1% of your day).
   - It seems to work **wonders** for anyone who merely experiments with it.
   - Results are often so dramatic that people typically refer to them as **miracles**!

2. **What benefits can I expect to derive from practicing this process?**

   Many experience an extraordinary sense of WELL-BEING the moment they indulge in their 15-Minute *←* Miracle. Most people love it because it causes them to feel GOOD about the PRESENT while looking FORWARD to the FUTURE. In short, this process is designed to offer you the GREATEST number of benefits, in the SHORTEST period of time, with the LEAST amount of effort! It makes it extremely easy for you to access the infinite wisdom and the abundant resources you ALREADY HAVE.

3. **Is the primary purpose of The 15-Minute *←* Miracle to manifest material things?**

   Although you are likely to experience many remarkable things as a result of practicing The 15-Minute *←* Miracle, material manifestations are really only BYPRODUCTS of doing this process. Because each step invites you to focus upon something that causes your energy to go UP, you begin to access the ability to stay in the flow of Life on a more CONSISTENT basis. When you achieve this state of mind, you begin to enjoy an ongoing state of GRATITUDE, which causes you to attract even MORE favorable conditions into your life. There are many inspiring testimonials starting on page 15 that will offer you enormous hope and encouragement. Even if only ONE person has successfully accomplished a particular thing, then YOU can do it TOO. If it has NEVER been done before, then YOU can be the FIRST!

43

4. **How long does it take before I am likely to see measurable results?**

    You are likely to experience positive effects the moment you engage in this process. You'll notice how good you feel RIGHT AWAY, which encourages you to KEEP doing it. Most people tell us that indulging in it an average of 5 TIMES A WEEK produces outstanding results (5 days on/2 days off). It is often only a short time before lots of little miracles begin to magically show up in your life on a regular basis, and it only gets BETTER from there!

5. **What does The 15-Minute ✳ Miracle primarily teach?**

    It teaches us how to easily CONNECT with our highest thought (JOY), our clearest word (TRUTH), our grandest feeling (LOVE), and our most cherished state of being (CONTENTMENT). Since Life communicates with us through our thoughts and feelings, we can learn to interpret them in ways that make it easy for us to stay on a SMOOTH and STEADY course. Think of it as a giant SMORGASBORD of creative ideas and SELECTIVELY fill your plate with whatever seems DELICIOUS to you!

6. **What makes it different from other self-help programs?**

    The biggest difference is the SIMPLICITY and ease with which a person can APPLY it and BENEFIT from it. Although many of the concepts and principles in this process seem familiar, many people tell us that they suddenly understand them on a much DEEPER level. Instead of merely showering people with KNOWLEDGE, it empowers them with WISDOM. Since wisdom is "knowledge applied," this is quite valuable. Because this process is SOLUTION ORIENTED, it is presented from a PURELY POSITIVE perspective. It naturally inspires a feeling of encouragement and positive anticipation. The basic principles behind The 15-Minute ✳ Miracle are certainly not new — only the EASE with which we can successfully integrate these ideas into our lives is unique.

7. **Is it anything like meditation?**

    Although it certainly renders many of the benefits of traditional meditation, it usually requires LESS time and is much MORE playful. People tell us that they love it because of its extremely user-friendly STRUCTURE. Like most folks, I was very eager to find ways to "follow my bliss" in the way Drs. Wayne Dyer and Deepak Chopra suggested. I longed to master the ancient art of meditation, but I had great difficulty in quieting my busy mind. Furthermore, I was totally unsuccessful at focusing upon my breathing and thinking of NOTHING. *The 15-Minute* ⤝ *Miracle* turned out to be a perfect way for me to meditate, because it only took 15 MINUTES a day for me to achieve an incredible sense of JOY and WELL-BEING on a consistent basis. It worked remarkably well, because I was able to consciously engage in something I enjoyed that measurably elevated my energy on ALL levels of my being. Not only was it FUN to do, but it also produced AMAZING RESULTS time and time again!

8.   **Can I learn this technique by just reading this book, or is it necessary to attend one of the Miracle ⤝ Mastery Playshops?**

It has been our experience that most ANYONE can learn this time-tested technique very quickly by merely reading this book and applying the simple principles. If, however, you wish to accelerate the rate at which you experience the kind of results that dreams are made of, you would greatly benefit from attending the weekend Playshops. Graduates commonly say, "It's fun to walk through each concept just ONE step at a time until you thoroughly understand the entire process. Because the Playshops are so EXPERIENTIAL, you have a lot of time to actually APPLY what you learn." These gatherings quickly empower you with the kind of self-awareness that allows you to consciously manifest SUSTAINED JOY and FEELINGS of BLISS into your life with incredible ease. Even MORE than that, they make it easy for you to become FULLY CONNECTED (and stay connected) to a glorious state of being that tends to take you BEYOND where you have ever been before. Attending a Playshop is like taking a delightful "Creation Vacation." It is always our personal goal to: 1) provide activities and tools that are FUN, 2) make things extremely SIMPLE, and 3) consistently EXCEED your wildest expectations. The only thing that we ask you to bring to any of our Miracle ⤝ Mastery Playshops is your DESIRE to be HAPPY. We'll provide the rest!

9.   **What exactly am I supposed to DO for 15 minutes a day?**

Just follow the format on pages 64-65 using the FIRST THOUGHTS (your intuition) that come into your awareness. You are bound to experience a measurably positive shift in your life when you practice this process regularly. As Ron and I always say,

"Positive shift happens…and it can happen to **YOU!"**

10.   What is the best time of day to engage in this process?

You can do your 15-Minute ⇥⇤ Miracle in the MORNING, in the EVENING, or ANYTIME in between. It is best, however, to get into the habit of doing it at the SAME time each day whenever possible. To DOUBLE your benefits, take time to READ whatever you have written just PRIOR to going to sleep. Better yet, AUDIOTAPE it and notice how you feel as you play it back. The most important thing is that you JUST DO IT. The SOONER you begin, the SOONER you'll enjoy the benefits!

11.   What is the best way to get started?

The easiest and most effective way to master The 15-Minute ⇥⇤ Miracle is to take full advantage of the valuable resources in the *Miracle Manifestation Manual*. This user-friendly companion book makes doing this process so much QUICKER and EASIER, because all you have to do is simply FILL IN THE BLANKS. You are welcome to COPY the examples in any of our books word for word until you become comfortable doing this process on your own. Think of them as TRAINING WHEELS that allow you to get up-and-running right away. If you truly want to MASTER this process, you may want to consider our **Deluxe Miracle Starter Kit**. It is the next best thing to attending one of our Miracle ⇥⇤ Mastery Playshops (for further information on products and event schedules, please check our website at www.15MinuteMiracle.com) or feel free to call us at (408) 353-2050.

12.   What if this process doesn't work for me?

We provide a **100% Satisfaction Guarantee** on absolutely everything we offer! If you faithfully practice this process in writing for at least 21 out of 30 days, and you can honestly say that the quality of your life has not MEASURABLY improved, simply return your materials and we will be happy to refund your money in full (please see our Satisfaction Guarantee on page 166). It is our ongoing intention to consistently EXCEED your wildest expectations!

Although today is the **first** day of the rest of my life,
I choose to enjoy it as though it were my **last**!

—Jacquelyn Aldana ⇥⇤ S.o.L.

Are you
singing the **song**
you came to **sing**?

—Joe and Judy Sabah

One of God's
greatest miracles is to
enable **ordinary** people to
do **extraordinary** things.

—H. Jackson Brown, Jr.

Part 3

Formula

...an exact **method**, **recipe**,
or **prescription** intended to
express a fundamental
truth or principle.

The 15-Minute ✳ Miracle
Success Formula

First focus upon your **ongoing intention**
then wipe your slate clean and claim a **new day**.

1. Write down all that you **appreciate** and **why**.

2. Explain how you most love to **feel** and **why**.

3. Summon divine guidance by **asking** questions.

4. Ask for **assistance** and **surrender** your fears.

5. Release and let go of anything negative.

6. Be **kind** to yourself or someone else.

7. Playfully bask in your **imagination**.

Now sign your **Sacred Contract**.

Benefits

... **advantages** that offer a sense of
well-being. Life continually offers a
multitude of benefits, but it is up to US to
become AWARE of them so that we can
gracefully INTEGRATE them into our
lives in ways that serve us well.

15 Benefits of Practicing
The 15-Minute ✦ Miracle

as expressed by our enthusiastic readers

It constantly inspires me to appreciate even the smallest of things!

It greatly improves relationships with my mate, co-workers, and friends!

It offers a foolproof formula for turning not-so-good days into great days!

It gives me permission to focus upon things that make me happy!

It provides abundant energy for me to do whatever I desire!

It gently guides me toward my highest purpose for being!

It makes me happy!

It improves my health!

It increases my wealth!

It amplifies my self-worth!

It makes me feel closer to God!

It empowers me with confidence!

It allows me to feel in charge of my life!

It lets me appreciate myself unconditionally!

It reminds me that Life is good and all is well!

If you **know**
what you **want**
you can **have** it!

—R.H.J. (author of *It Works*)

Let's Tune in to ✳ **wiii FM**

(**W**hat **is in it F**or **M**e?)

When you consistently practice 𝔗𝔥𝔢 15-Minute ✳ Miracle, you are likely to fe-e-e-e-el...

_ accomplished	_ desirable	_ inspired	_ resourceful
_ adventurous	_ dynamic	_ intuitive	_ romantic
_ affluent	_ elated	_ inventive	_ satisfied
_ animated	_ empowered	_ invigorated	_ secure
_ appreciated	_ energetic	_ jovial	_ self-assured
_ articulate	_ enlightened	_ joyful	_ self-confident
_ attractive	_ enthusiastic	_ lighthearted	_ serene
_ aware	_ evolved	_ loving	_ special
_ balanced	_ excited	_ mentally sharp	_ spirited
_ beautiful	_ exhilarated	_ motivated	_ spiritual
_ blissful	_ exuberant	_ optimistic	_ spontaneous
_ calm	_ flexible	_ passionate	_ steady
_ capable	_ focused	_ peaceful	_ talented
_ carefree	_ fortunate	_ physically fit	_ triumphant
_ clear	_ free	_ playful	_ unstoppable
_ clever	_ fulfilled	_ positive	_ versatile
_ comfortable	_ grateful	_ powerful	_ vital
_ complete	_ happy	_ productive	_ vivacious
_ content	_ harmonious	_ proficient	_ wholesome
_ courageous	_ healthy	_ progressive	_ wise
_ creative	_ humorous	_ prosperous	_ worthy
_ delighted	_ independent	_ receptive	_ youthful

Soon you will **smile** as you hear yourself say,
"It's just the story of my life! **More** of this, please!"

55

IT is your
Inner Teacher,
Invisible Therapist,
as well as your InTuition

—Jacquelyn Aldana ⭐ S.o.L.

"IT" is Your ✳← Best Friend

𝕿𝖍𝖊 15-𝓜𝖎𝖓𝖚𝖙𝖊 ✳← 𝓜𝖎𝖗𝖆𝖈𝖑𝖊 teaches us how to effectively communicate with our Inner Teacher (affectionately known as **IT**). **IT** is that internal voice that speaks to us to offer guidance from time to time. It is easy to recognize this voice, because **IT** consistently urges us to MOVE FORWARD toward our highest purpose for being. **IT** is essentially the same as our **InT**uition. Someone once told me that **InT**uition is actually GOD speaking to us between our thoughts. If this is true, we may want to talk a little LESS and listen a lot MORE!

Life cleverly communicates with us through our visceral feelings of COMFORT and DISCOMFORT. Sometimes we get messages in the form of IMAGES in our minds, while at other times we experience a strong "GUT feeling" in our solar plexus. If you want to strengthen your sense of **InT**uition, pay very close attention to the way you FE-E-E-EL about things. The more you consciously NOTICE "how you are feeling" and "what you are experiencing," the easier it will be for you to recognize and TRUST your magnificent Inner Guidance System.

You'll be glad to know that EVERY situation offers a BENEFIT of some kind. As it turns out, it is actually a BLESSING when you experience that twinge of negative emotion from time to time. It's only Life alerting you that you are TEMPORARILY out of harmony with your desires. This is your cue to immediately REDIRECT your attention to something (anything) that you APPRECIATE. A simple sense of gratitude inspires you to feel encouraged right away. When you realize that your Inner Teacher is merely prompting you to focus upon things that make you happy, you will be able to more easily ACCEPT whatever Life offers you REGARDLESS of circumstances. When you discover how to effectively communicate with **IT**…

You'll soon be able to transform your

fondest **dreams** into your most cherished **realities**!

Once we discover how we UNKNOWINGLY attract undesirable circumstances into our lives, we can then CONSCIOUSLY call forth the quality of life we PREFER to experience instead. Simple APPRECIATION and FOCUS are the primary keys to personal fulfillment — appreciating what we ALREADY HAVE coupled with focusing upon how we PREFER to feel.

Once again, it's all about learning to work in HARMONY with one of the most powerful laws in the Universe — the Law of Magnetic Attraction.

At first, you may be somewhat SKEPTICAL of this "sounds-too-good-to-be-true" process. We can't say that we blame you. Because it's so SIMPLE, it's hard to imagine how it could actually work SO QUICKLY and with SO LITTLE EFFORT. We certainly don't expect you to totally comprehend the power of 𝕿he 15-Minute ⭐ Miracle until you actually DO IT and EXPERIENCE IT for yourself. Once you see what happens, you will better understand why so many people have become so fascinated with it. After all, **"seeing is believing."** Thousands of people around the world who have already experienced the magic of this intriguing "phenomenology" have exclaimed with great enthusiasm,

"IT works! IT really works!"

That's why we have every reason to believe that **IT** will work for YOU as well. As you read this book, you will see the word **"IT"** many times. Every time you see or hear this word, please remember what **IT** really is. **IT** is the Divine Presence within you that creates the conscious awareness of the infinite possibilities that are available to you — **IT** is your **Inner Teacher** and/or **Invisible Therapist** (whichever you prefer) who absolutely adores you. And best of all…

IT is always with you.

The only time **IT** APPEARS to be absent is when you are focused upon PROBLEMS or indulging in SELF-PITY. In other words, when you are NEGATIVELY FOCUSED, **IT** seems nowhere to be found. When you decide to TAKE CHARGE of your life and begin to look for SOLUTIONS, **IT** will follow you everywhere! The funny thing is this: The MORE you freely enjoy **IT** and have fun with **IT**, the BETTER **IT** works. You might like to playfully think of **IT** as **"The Genie Within."**

What Do You Really
Need to Be ✳ **Happy**?

To keep this process LIGHT and FUN, Ron suggested I provide you with tools that will make "getting started" extremely easy. To find out what people had to say on the subject of HAPPINESS, we decided to conduct a survey. The majority of the folks we interviewed felt they definitely needed to obtain THREE main things before they could even BEGIN to be happy. They typically said:

"WHEN I have **permission,**

WHEN I have enough **time,** and

WHEN I get **around to it,** THEN I'll be happy."

We often limit ourselves because we BELIEVE we require these three things before we can experience a true sense of well-being. A shortcut to realizing your dreams and desires is to simply give YOURSELF permission to do the things you love most — things that generate life-force energy, boost your immune system, and cause you to leap out of bed in the morning with unstoppable enthusiasm! When you do what you honestly ENJOY, then LOVE, PROSPERITY, and MIRACLES eagerly follow you around as though you were the Pied Piper. By all appearances, this is one of Life's best-kept secrets!

If you relate to any of the above "reasons why I can't enjoy life now," you have come to the right place! Included in this book (at no extra charge) are ALL THREE THINGS you need in order to take quantum leaps into a happier, more fulfilling life. Feel free to use these tools as often as you like. They are good for an entire lifetime, so take advantage of them frequently. Go ahead:

Allow yourself to be **playful** and have **fun** with them!

Happiness ✳ Survival Kit

✳ Permission Slip

Unconditional **permission is now granted** hereby enabling you to **feel free to…**

__ Goof off	__ Take a day off	__ Spend money on yourself
__ Take a nap	__ Listen to music	__ Eat whenever you want to
__ Laugh a lot	__ Take a vacation	__ Take time out just for you
__ Fall in love	__ Go to bed early	__ Honestly say what you feel
__ Take a walk	__ Appreciate yourself	__ Treat yourself to a massage
__ Take a break	__ Have fun and be happy	__ Sleep in until you feel rested
__ Read a book	__ Spend quiet time alone	__ Take time to do nothing at all
__ Watch a movie	__ Lighten up and enjoy life	__ Meditate and think of nothing
__ Breathe deeply	__ Release, let go, and relax	__ Do your 15-Minute ✳ Miracle

Note: You are **entitled to receive** only as much permission as you are **willing to accept**.

Void if accompanied by Guilt, Fear, or Anxiety!   Permission Slip expires when you do!

✳ Valuable Coupon

This coupon entitles the bearer to **15 Minutes a day**
for the purpose of attracting and **creating miracles.**
This time is reserved exclusively for **YOU,** and **only YOU!**
It is guaranteed ☺ **Guilt-Free,** ☺ **Fat-Free,** and ☺ **Totally Legal!**

✳ A ROUND TUIT

Now **YOU** can **DO IT!**

Part 4

✦ 15 Minutes

...the average time it takes to
do your 15-Minute ✦ Miracle. In
less than **1% of your day**, you can
easily pave the way to become an
"Irresistible Magnet for Miracles!"

Overview of the
15-Minute ✳ Miracle™ Process

Ongoing Intention: By mastering just ONE ongoing intention a day, you can easily create a whole NEW and IMPROVED "Story of Your Life!"

Clean Slate: This segment reminds you that you have been granted another BRAND NEW DAY to enjoy "singing the song you came here to sing." Ah-h-h-h...Life is so-o-o-o good!

Step #1-Appreciation: This step opens the door for all the OTHER steps to attract miracles into your life. Explaining WHY you are thankful greatly DEEPENS the effect of this process.

Step #2-Feel-Good: This step sets a POSITIVE TONE for your day, so be sure to do it in its entirety. It is at least 10 TIMES more powerful when you complete ALL THREE SEGMENTS.

Step #3-Get Intuit: This step develops your power of INTUITION and makes it easy for you to access answers to your questions, solutions to your problems, and pieces to your puzzle.

Step #4-Power: This step invites you to call upon your Higher Power for DIVINE ASSISTANCE as you completely SURRENDER all worries, doubts, and fears.

Step #5-Freedom: This step FREES you to live a higher quality of Life by letting go of all issues (both known and unknown) that no longer serve you (or anyone else) in a positive way.

Step #6-Kindness: This step brings out your HIGHEST NATURE while elevating your sense of SELF-WORTH. Kindness toward ANYONE benefits EVERYONE — especially YOU!

Step #7-Tell-A-Vision: Tell me your VISION and I'll tell you your FUTURE! This step enables you to set up a fulfilling life for yourself based upon what you playfully IMAGINE.

My Sacred Contract-This is a FORMAL AGREEMENT between YOU and LIFE. By signing it, you signify that you are willing to ACCEPT all the GOODNESS that Life wants you to have.

NOTE: Steps 1-3 constitute the **BASIC VERSION** of The 15-Minute ✳ Miracle.
Steps 4-7 are called the **ADDED POWER BOOST STEPS** and are completely optional.

My 15-Minute ✳ Miracle™

Day 1 ✳ Appreciation

Starting today, my **ongoing intention** is to
express GRATITUDE for even the SMALLEST of things.

Today *(Day/Date)*   Thursday, June 27, 2002   **is a CLEAN SLATE for me to enjoy!** 👍

1.   **I am so fortunate, BECAUSE Life always blesses me with MORE of whatever I sincerely appreciate.**

Today, I really APPRECIATE my close friends, **BECAUSE** they always encourage me to speak from my HEART and follow my DREAMS.

I am so GRATEFUL for my husband Ron, **BECAUSE** he fully SUPPORTS me in all that I choose to do. After nearly 30 years, he is still my BEST FRIEND and the LOVE of MY LIFE.

I am so GRATEFUL that I have the ability to CHOOSE my thoughts, **BECAUSE** it allows me to consistently tap into the very BEST that Life has to offer.

2.   **I love it when I FEEL** happy.

WHEN I feel this way, THEN I am able to APPRECIATE how very FORTUNATE I am,
which makes it EASY for me to naturally view Life from a more POSITIVE PERSPECTIVE.

3.   **My primary intention for today is to receive a CLEAR ANSWER to the following QUESTION:**

What can I do to have more FUN and enjoy a HIGHER quality of life?

ANSWERS that came into my awareness when I asked the above question:

- WRITE down everything you APPRECIATE and state WHY you are grateful.
- CLARIFY your desires by doing your 15-Minute ✳ Miracle on a REGULAR BASIS.
- APPRECIATE even the SMALLEST of things and look for the BENEFITS in every situation.

4. I now invite ASSISTANCE from *The Loving Power* I recognize as greater than myself:

Thank You __God__ for Your perfect guidance, unconditional love, and ongoing support. If it is in the highest good for me and for All Life Everywhere, please DIVINELY ORCHESTRATE the following in just the perfect time:

- Help me to always be in the RIGHT PLACE at the RIGHT TIME.
- Show me FUN and EASY ways to achieve my PERFECT body weight and size.
- Assist ALL of our clients and friends to become "Irresistible MAGNETS for Miracles."

I completely SURRENDER all worries, doubts, and fears to You __God__. When I entrust YOU to take care of the details, everything falls into place for ME with amazing ease.

5. I am now READY and WILLING to RELEASE and LET GO of my RESISTANCE to change,

plus ALL issues both known and unknown that no longer serve me in a positive way, which FREES me to LIVE fully, LOVE deeply, and LAUGH often.

6. My special way of being KIND to _____my beloved Ron_____ today is to get up extra early and prepare a SCRUMPTIOUS BREAKFAST for him to have in BED when he wakes up.

7. Since I can *be, do,* and *have* absolutely ANYTHING, I see myself ALREADY enjoying the following:

- I am more FIT, TRIM, and STRONG than I have ever been in my entire life!
- I have plenty of TIME to engage in the creative things that I most enjoy doing!
- I totally LOVE whatever I'm doing whenever I'm doing it. Life is so much FUN!
- I enjoy multiple streams of RESIDUAL INCOME that enable me to make all of my decisions based solely upon DESIRE. I am extraordinarily blessed!

With enormous GRATITUDE, I now agree to ACCEPT these and even GREATER gifts in just the PERFECT TIME in DELIGHTFUL WAYS that express the HIGHEST GOOD for All Life Everywhere.

Signed... *Jacquelyn Aldana*   Date... *June 27, 2002*

I am an "Irresistible Magnet for Miracles!" It's just the story of my life! MORE of this, please!
(*Listen as Life whispers in your ear...*"You're RIGHT! Let me show you MORE EVIDENCE of this!")

Write 'Em and Reap

Studies have consistently shown that those who WRITE down their dreams and desires achieve their goals more frequently than those who just THINK about them. Because we have over 60,000 thoughts racing through our minds each day (85% of which we probably thought about yesterday), it is best to focus only upon the thoughts that MATCH our desires. After all, "What you THINK ABOUT is what you BRING ABOUT," so why not bring about things that enable you to THRIVE and PROSPER? If for any reason writing is too time consuming or difficult for you, then simply record your daily 15-Minute ✴ Miracle on an audiocassette. It yields extremely positive results and it usually takes LESS TIME than writing.

You'll be glad to know that The 15-Minute ✴ Miracle works for most ANYONE who is merely willing to EXPERIMENT with it. When you invest just 15 MINUTES A DAY to playfully indulge in this process, the other 23 hours and 45 minutes seem to fall into place with much greater EASE and GRACE. For every 15 minutes you INVEST in paving the way for a magnificent day, you probably SAVE countless hours, days, weeks, months...even years that it might otherwise take you to even come CLOSE to fulfilling your dreams.

For optimum results, we recommend that you do this process in writing for at least 5 DAYS A WEEK for the next month until you have done it for a minimum of 21 DAYS. Whatever you can do for 21 days is likely to become a COMFORTABLE HABIT. After a while, however, you may not even be able to get to the PAPER fast enough before things magically begin to MANIFEST into your life (sometimes at the speed of thought)! It is also very important that you make the correlation between what you WRITE and what you EXPERIENCE. When you realize that YOU are the one creating the MAGIC or the MISERY in your life, you can experience YOUR version of Life in ways that are much more FUN.

To increase the odds of your success even MORE, invest a few minutes at the END of your day to make a note of all the synchronistic events that "just miraculously showed up" in your life. Either create a "Record of Miracles" on a separate sheet of paper or use the special section in the back of your *Miracle Manifestation Manual* entitled "My Miracle Collection."

This shows you what you have been ATTRACTING and CREATING on a daily basis and it reminds you of how SUCCESSFUL you have become. It also enables you to make the CONNECTION between what you THINK ABOUT and what you actually BRING ABOUT. You will find it extremely revealing. Once you realize how CAPABLE and POWERFUL you really are, you are bound to feel more IN CHARGE of your life. If you're like most of us, you'll begin to wonder how you ever made it through your life this far without knowing about 𝕿𝔥𝔢 15-𝓜𝔦𝔫𝔲𝔱𝔢 →←𝓜𝔦𝔯𝔞𝔠𝔩𝔢.

Have you ever said to yourself, "There's just got to be a BETTER WAY to play this game of Life?" Here's GOOD NEWS for you: We believe that the "better way" is right here, RIGHT NOW and is ready for you to utilize IMMEDIATELY! In the section that follows, we will reveal **7 simple steps** that are designed to make it extremely easy for you to go beyond where you have ever gone before. Our primary intention is to thoroughly explain each step of 𝕿𝔥𝔢 15-𝓜𝔦𝔫𝔲𝔱𝔢 →←𝓜𝔦𝔯𝔞𝔠𝔩𝔢 in ways that are EASY for you to understand and FUN for you to use. If you are like the thousands of others who have experimented with this remarkable formula, you are likely to EXCEED your wildest expectations in less time than you would imagine. So fasten your seat belt and get ready to "SOAR with EAGLES and FLY with ANGELS!"

Ongoing Intention

...a clear **declaration** of what one
has in mind to do or bring about.
Intentions prime the pump for
wishes to become realities.

The Road to Success is Paved with ✳ Ongoing Intentions

Taking action **prior** to creating a **clear intention** is like
putting on a **blindfold** and riding a **runaway horse** with **no reins**!

—Jacquelyn Aldana ✳ S.o.L.

Day 1 ✳ Appreciation

Starting today, my **ongoing intention is** to
express GRATITUDE for even the SMALLEST of things.

Reading or creating a positive ONGOING INTENTION prior to filling in the blanks of your 15-Minute ✳ Miracle is a WISE and WONDERFUL way to start your day. Each one of these POWERFUL DECLARATIONS will impact your mind and open your heart to enjoy a state of being that most people only read about in BOOKS or see in MOVIES. If you are using the preprinted forms in the *Miracle Manifestation Manual* (the companion to this book), you will have access to more than 60 different ongoing intentions that are designed to quickly ACCELERATE the rate at which "The Miracle Process" works for YOU. Because the *Miracle Manifestation Manual* is a convenient "2-month fill-in-the-blanks journal" as well as a "results-oriented activity book," it offers literally HUNDREDS of examples for you to copy WORD for WORD. These examples are the "BEST of the BEST" of everything that has proven to work wonders in the lives of thousands. They make doing this process as easy as PAINTING by NUMBERS.

If you truly desire to become an "Irresistible Magnet For Miracles" in the SHORTEST period of time and with the LEAST amount of effort, you will want to not only READ these daily ongoing intentions, but you will also want to MEMORIZE and MASTER them! What took me well over a half century to learn, YOU can now master in only a month or two by claiming every one of these powerful intentions for yourself. Each ongoing intention invites you to ALIGN the focus of your attention with your dreams and desires in ways that summon results that are bound to AMAZE and DELIGHT you!

✦ Clean Slate

Invite **fresh starts** and
second chances by wiping your
mental slate clean each day to
make room for delightful
new beginnings!

Write the Date ⋇ Clean Your Slate

The past is **history**, the future is a **mystery**,

but today is a **gift**. This is why we call it **"The present!"**

—Author Unknown

Today *(Day/Date)* _____ Thursday, June 27, 2002 _____ **is a CLEAN SLATE for me to enjoy!**

One of the most precious gifts that Life provides each one of us is the opportunity to start each new day with a fresh CLEAN SLATE. We are so fortunate to be granted yet another day to experience Life with the "wisdom of yesterday" coupled with the "dreams of today." If one of your goals is to become "The Happiest Person You Know," this particular segment of 𝕿𝖍𝖊 15-𝕸𝖎𝖓𝖚𝖙𝖊 ⋇ 𝕸𝖎𝖗𝖆𝖈𝖑𝖊 process is absolutely ESSENTIAL for you to practice daily.

Embrace each day as though it were the FIRST day of your HONEYMOON and the LAST day of your VACATION! Discard the negativity of the past and focus exclusively upon what you PREFER to experience from this day forward. You can easily accomplish this by entertaining only PURELY POSITIVE THOUGHTS. If, however, you feel the need to discuss things you DON'T LIKE, things you DON'T WANT, and things you want to GET RID OF, do yourself a huge favor. Be sure to PREFACE any statements of negativity with **"In the past..."** or **"Up until now..."** By remembering to employ this simple practice, you no longer foolishly invite UNWANTED things and events into your PRESENT or FUTURE. For example:

In the past, I have felt extremely OVERWHELMED. From now on,
I prefer to experience more CONTENTMENT, PEACE, and JOY in my life.

Remembering this valuable tip promises to FREE you from the burdens of yesterday more quickly. Although this time-tested technique is very SIMPLE, it is extremely POWERFUL. Not only is creating a clean slate each day an important part of 𝕿𝖍𝖊 15-𝕸𝖎𝖓𝖚𝖙𝖊 ⋇ 𝕸𝖎𝖗𝖆𝖈𝖑𝖊, but it is also one of the FIRST STEPS in becoming an "Irresistible Magnet for Miracles."

✦ Appreciation

...grateful **recognition** of one's
blessings and a warm expression
of **praise**, **admiration**, and **approval**.
When we express heartfelt appreciation
for all that we ALREADY HAVE, we invite
Life to provide many MORE wondrous
things for which to be grateful!

Step #1
The ✴ Appreciation Step

Miracles are happening **everywhere** all the time,
but only those with an **"Attitude of Gratitude"** seem to notice them.

—Author Unknown

I am so fortunate, BECAUSE Life always blesses me with MORE of whatever I appreciate.

Today, I really APPRECIATE those who call to SHARE their miracles, **BECAUSE** they make it easier for others to BELIEVE that miracles are also possible for THEM.

I am so GRATEFUL for my HEALTH, **BECAUSE** it allows me to pursue my dreams with VITALITY.

The Appreciation Step is the first step in **The 15-Minute ✴ Miracle** process for a very specific reason. It is NUMBER ONE because it opens the door for all the OTHER steps to work to our greatest advantage. Instead of just making a typical "gratitude list," this step asks us to explain WHY we are grateful. As we ponder our blessings in this way, we can't help but DEEPEN our sense of appreciation, which makes us realize how very FORTUNATE we are ALREADY. Some people feel they are able to access a more PROFOUND sense of appreciation by using the word GRATITUDE. If this is true for you, simply rephrase this step as follows: **"I am so GRATEFUL...BECAUSE..."** Gratitude is the magic BRIDGE to a more sustainable sense of JOY, and joy is the KEY to becoming "The Happiest Person You Know."

We find that most people who are drawn to **The 15-Minute ✴ Miracle** are in a state of LONGING and YEARNING for things to be different in their lives. As it turns out, most of them either WANT something they don't HAVE or HAVE something they don't WANT (or both). Unfortunately, in their state of NEEDING and PLEADING, they unknowingly attract MORE of the very things they DON'T WANT — more LACK, limitation, and not having! For a more fulfilling life, we recommend that you make it your ongoing intention to...

Transform all longing, yearning, and **needing** into
appreciation, gratitude, and **succeeding**.

Appreciation Saved Our Marriage!

The stress of struggling to make ends meet and trying to keep Ron alive for three years began to completely overwhelm both of us. EVERYTHING in our lives began to fall apart, including our 20-year marriage! A health practitioner friend of mine suggested that I go to a quiet place and write down everything that I APPRECIATED about Ron. It took me quite some time to release my resistance and resentment long enough to write anything very complimentary. Once I got started, however, I wrote SEVERAL PAGES of glowing comments about the man I had married 20 years before. Although I never showed it to him, nor did he ever read it, the very next morning Ron responded to me with enormous warmth and tenderness. As a result, all hostilities and misgivings completely DISSOLVED. Only 12 HOURS after I did this little writing exercise, our failing relationship was completely HEALED and our love for each other was GREATER than ever before. This was truly a miracle when you consider the fact that we barely spoke for nearly EIGHT MONTHS. In my opinion, APPRECIATION is to WELL-BEING what OXYGEN is to BREATHING!

Gratitude Saved Ron's Life!

When Ron was suffering from cancer, he found it very difficult to appreciate much of ANYTHING. Finally, one day after the doctors said that he might not even make it through the night, he made the decision to do something DIFFERENT. Because he wanted to make the MOST of whatever time he had left, he consciously turned his attention from DEATH, DYING, and DEVASTATION to LIFE, LIVING, and LOVING every moment he had left. **The most amazing thing happened!** He not only made it through the NIGHT, but he also began to feel a bit better the following DAY. As he celebrated another glorious day, he experienced a little MORE STRENGTH and ENCOURAGEMENT. After a few more days, he was finally released from the hospital. Ron faithfully wrote his 15-Minute ⇥← Miracle every day for THREE MONTHS then returned for his regular checkup. The doctors were utterly DUMBFOUNDED! After a plethora of tests, they could not find even a TRACE of cancer anywhere in his body. They pronounced him totally CANCER FREE! Although the doctors called it a "spontaneous remission," Ron and I KNOW that it was nothing short of a MIRACLE!

We Always Get MORE of Whatever We Appreciate!

Things for which we express LOVE, GRATITUDE, and SINCERE APPRECIATION naturally **expand**. Life humorously emulates my beloved grandmother when she used to serve the evening meal. If I complimented her on a particular dish that she had lovingly prepared, she would INSTANTLY provide me with SECOND HELPINGS. Life does exactly the same thing — It always makes sure we get MORE of whatever we LOVE and APPRECIATE!

Benefits of Appreciation

- It only has **positive** side effects.

- It provides a delightful **shortcut** to miracles.

- It floods your body with **immune-boosting endorphins**.

- It puts you back into the **flow of Life** at the speed of thought.

- It is the lantern that shines the **brightest light** in your darkest hour.

- It provides a totally legal way for you to enjoy a "**natural high**."

- It causes you to feel a wonderful sense of "**coming home**."

- It provides an immediate sense of **well-being**.

- It is the main cause of "**sustained joy**."

Shortcuts to Manifestation

The quickest and easiest way to transform your WISHES into REALITIES is to consciously appreciate what you ALREADY HAVE before asking for MORE. Herein lies the key to success and personal fulfillment. Focus upon what IS working in your life and what IS right with the world, no matter how SMALL or seemingly INSIGNIFICANT it may be. Before long, MORE things will fall into place with little or NO EFFORT on your part. Because you cannot possibly experience negative emotion when you are expressing GRATITUDE, it is a wonderful tool to use when you want to FEEL GOOD in a HURRY!

✦ Feelings

… physical or emotional **responses** that are marked by **sensations** of comfort or discomfort. COMFORT means we are "in the flow of Life." DISCOMFORT indicates that Life is inviting us to focus upon what we PREFER to feel instead.

Step #2
The Feel-Good Step

It is not words, but rather the **feelings behind the words** that possess the magnetic force that transforms our **fondest dreams** into our most **cherished realities**.

—Jacquelyn Aldana S.o.L.

I love it when **I FEEL** totally PEACEFUL.

WHEN I feel this way, **THEN** I am able to completely RELAX,

which makes it EASY for me to stay focused upon everything I LOVE and APPRECIATE.

Isn't it amazing how our mouths begin to water the moment we even IMAGINE sucking on a tart juicy lemon? The very same principle applies when we merely ENVISION ourselves FE-E-E-E-ELING a particular way. By making a statement like, "I love it when I feel PLAYFUL," we cause our entire physiology to experience feelings of playfulness at the speed of thought. Since our thoughts are the CAUSE of our experiences and we get to CHOOSE our thoughts, we also get to CHOOSE our PREFERRED STATE OF BEING. It appears that Life communicates with us through POSITIVE and NEGATIVE EMOTION:

>**Positive emotion** feels **GOOD** and offers us a sense of **comfort**.
>**Negative emotion** feels **BAD** and offers us a sense of **discomfort**.

Our feelings are like GAUGES on the dashboard of an automobile. Both are INDICATORS of what is going on inside (under the hood so to speak). They let us know when it is time to REFUEL or make necessary ADJUSTMENTS in order to keep everything running SMOOTHLY. That's why it is extremely important for us to pay very close ATTENTION to our FEELINGS. When we experience COMFORT, our energy is UP and we know we are "in the flow." When we feel a sense of DISCOMFORT, our energy dwindles and we feel a bit off balance. Normally we think of discomfort as being negative, but as it turns out,

This is actually a **good** thing!

NEGATIVE EMOTIONS simply let us know that our gauges are working PERFECTLY. They are just alerting us that we are TEMPORARILY out of harmony with our desires. When we feel the sensation of COMFORT, we are enjoying the energy of **LOVE**, which is an acronym for **L**iving **O**n **V**elvet **E**nergy. When we feel DISCOMFORT, we experience the energy of **FEAR**, which is just a clever acronym for **F**orgetting **E**verything's **A**ll **R**ight! When you want to quickly RECONNECT with a sense of COMFORT, simply find something (anything) to APPRECIATE and you will be able to RETURN to your "stream of well-being" almost immediately. As we indicated before, "Appreciation is your LIFELINE to well-being."

While positive thinking is essential for positive outcomes, it is actually the power of POSITIVE FEELING that provides the magnetic force that shapes our DESTINY. According to the HeartMath Institute in Boulder Creek, California, "The PHYSICAL HEART generates 60 TIMES more electrical energy than the PHYSICAL BRAIN." That's why we feel such a surge of ENERGY when we finally muster up the courage to speak from our HEARTS and express how we truly feel. The energy of EMPOWERMENT is a natural byproduct of AUTHENTICITY.

Are you consciously AWARE of how you feel? Sometimes, as a result of suffering deep emotional pain, we unknowingly distance ourselves from our feelings as a way of temporarily COPING with Life. Unfortunately, when we numb our feelings of PAIN, we also numb our feelings of JOY. The benefit in allowing ourselves to feel ALL of our feelings (both positive and negative) is that we can then CHOOSE which ones to KEEP and which ones to RELEASE! Fortunately, WE get to make these choices. If you are now ready to move beyond yesterday's fears and disappointments, you can declare that TODAY is a brand new day to start off fresh and you can begin to claim the GOODNESS that Life is so eager for you to have.

If you are NOT READY at this time, that's OKAY too. Perhaps you are grieving the loss of something or someone in your life. If so, it is essential that you HONOR your feelings and give yourself TOTAL PERMISSION to GRIEVE for as long as you need to. It is equally important, however, to set a SPECIFIC DATE when you are ready and willing to MOVE FORWARD in your life (otherwise, the grieving process can literally rob you of joy FOREVER). A friend of mine who was absolutely DEVASTATED from the fallout of a failed relationship called me one day to ask for help. Rather than trying to cheer him up, this is what I said:

"Give yourself total permission to FEEL your feelings and express your grief for as long as you need to, then determine a specific date when you feel you will be ready to go beyond where you are right now." After giving it a lot of thought, he decided to give himself a full SIX WEEKS to grieve. Three days later he called me back and said, "I did exactly what you suggested. I totally immersed myself in my profound feelings of devastation and disappointment night and day for the last three days. I now feel totally COMPLETE with it and I am ready to start moving on with my life!" Since he used to suffer from chronic depression, he was amazed at how FAST he was able to successfully process this issue using this methodology. As soon as he began doing his 15-Minute ✳ Miracle again, things began to fall into place for him in ways that matched his visions. Today, he is HAPPIER, HEALTHIER, and more PROSPEROUS than ever before. The next time you feel off balance, instead of putting on the "smile of denial," give yourself full PERMISSION to fe-e-e-e-el your feelings (ALL of them), then set a SPECIFIC DATE when you think you will be ready to MOVE ON.

How to be Happy Right NOW

HAVE FUN REMINISCING IN YOUR PLEASANT PAST: Recall a special day in your life when you felt EXCEPTIONALLY happy, then notice how you FE-E-E-E-EL in your body as you begin to RE-EXPERIENCE all of the same wonderful sensations that you so enjoyed in the past. Now think of as many adjectives as you can to describe how you feel RIGHT NOW. Because my pleasant memories make me feel good just to THINK about them, I make a point to keep them in the FOREFRONT of my mind so I can easily ACCESS them whenever I choose to.

PONDER THE POSITIVE POSSIBILITIES OF THE FUTURE: Now think about something you are really looking FORWARD to in the future. Again, notice how you FEEL in your body as you allow yourself to succumb to the exhilaration of positive anticipation. Using just one-word adjectives, describe how you feel RIGHT NOW. If you are like most people, you will feel a wonderful sense of POSITIVE EXPECTANCY about good things coming your way. Your entire body, mind, and spirit will benefit immensely from this simple activity. We suggest that you repeat this process until you FE-E-E-E-EL a measurable degree of positive emotion.

To make it even EASIER for you to feel uplifted and encouraged as you learn to master this "Feel-Good Step," we have provided a handy **Happiness Dictionary** on the next page.

When I am HAPPY, I feel...

A	G	M	S
Ageless	Gifted	Magical	Super
Amazing	Graceful	Motivated	Satisfied
Awesome	Genuine	Marvelous	Successful
Abundant	Generous	Miraculous	Sensational
Appreciated	Grounded	Magnificent	Stupendous
B	**H**	**N**	**T**
Blissful	Honest	New	Terrific
Blessed	Healthy	Nice	Tickled
Balanced	Hilarious	Needed	Trusting
Beautiful	Humorous	Noticed	Talented
Bountiful	Harmonious	Nourished	Tremendous
C	**I**	**O**	**U**
Clear	Inspired	Open	Unique
Content	Intuitive	Opulent	Uplifted
Creative	Inventive	Outgoing	Unlimited
Confident	Ingenious	Optimistic	Unbeatable
Connected	Insightful	Outrageous	Unstoppable
D	**J**	**P**	**V**
Daring	Jolly	Positive	Valued
Decisive	Jovial	Pleasant	Valiant
Dynamic	Joyful	Peaceful	Vigorous
Deserving	Jazzed	Powerful	Vivacious
Delighted	Jubilant	Passionate	Victorious
E	**K**	**Q**	**W**
Elated	Kind	Quiet	Wise
Ecstatic	Kissable	Quick	Witty
Energetic	Knowing	Quixotic	Worthy
Exhilarated	Kind-Hearted	Qualified	Wealthy
Empowered	Knowledgeable	Quintessential	Wonderful
F	**L**	**R**	**X, Y, Z**
Free	Light	Rich	Young
Friendly	Lucky	Radiant	Youthful
Fantastic	Loving	Relaxed	Zany
Fortunate	Luminous	Renewed	Zestful
Fun-Loving	Light-hearted	Refreshed	Zealous

Go Back to your DIVINE SOURCE

Imagine yourself as a beautiful long-stemmed glass filled with sparkling CRYSTAL CLEAR WATER from the PUREST SOURCE in the Universe. When you hold it up to the light, it is easy to see tiny bubbles dancing as they celebrate their EFFERVESCENCE. This is a simple metaphor that describes the degree of LIGHT and PERFECTION with which you came into your physical existence. The pristine water in the glass represents YOU when you are in the FLOW of Life appreciating even the smallest of things — YOU when you are HAPPY and GRATEFUL for what you ALREADY have while looking forward to even MORE wonderful things.

If you are like most people, however, you probably experience times that are LESS than ideal. Allowing yourself to become negatively focused for very long is equivalent to putting a drop of BLACK INK into your glass. If you keep looking at what's NOT WORKING, what you DON'T LIKE, and what you want to GET RID OF, your sparkling glass of pure, clean water will soon become quite MURKY. You are likely to become DISCOURAGED and OVERWHELMED trying to find ways to extract all those yucky black molecules out of the water. Is it even possible? How would you do it? Where would you start?

The answer is so simple and yet it works at the SPEED of THOUGHT! Instead of struggling to remove the darkness, simply RECONNECT with your Divine Source. Just place your glass under the faucet of LOVE and LIGHT and allow the pure magnificence of LIFE to fill your glass to overflowing, thereby completely DISPLACING the darkness of negativity and REPLACING it with the light of love. Since Step #2 (The Feel-Good Step) invites us to CHOOSE how we love to FEEL, we can CHOOSE to feel in the flow of Life in every moment. Choosing to focus upon feelings of LOVE, JOY, and APPRECIATION is like inviting the Red Sea to part, thereby making it POSSIBLE for us to reach that long-awaited "shore of fulfillment."

✳ Intuit

...to gain valuable insights
through our power of **intuition**
thereby tapping into infinite
knowledge and wisdom.

Step #3

The Get Intuit Step

If you want to know what's really **true**,
just hear the voice inside of **you**.

—Jacquelyn Aldana ⨳ S.o.L.

My primary intention for today is to receive a CLEAR ANSWER to the following QUESTION:

How can I create a more harmonious relationship with _____ ?

ANSWERS that came into my awareness when I asked the above question:

♥ Make a written list of all of the POSITIVE THINGS that you like about this person.

♥ Bring out this person's HIGHEST NATURE by telling him or her what you LIKE about them.

♥ Communicate freely with him or her by speaking your TRUTH right from your HEART.

How to Get LIFE to Reveal Its Most Valuable SECRETS

• Ask a SPECIFIC QUESTION and request a crystal CLEAR RESPONSE.

• Write the very first UNCENSORED thoughts that flow into your awareness.

• Take appropriate ACTION based upon the information (or inspiration) you receive.

Wouldn't it be nice if we had a full-time MENTOR to call upon 24/7 (24 hours a day/7 days a week)? Wouldn't it be comforting to be able to ask QUESTIONS and receive ANSWERS at the speed of THOUGHT? Wouldn't it be great to have a source of good advice that enabled us to make WISE DECISIONS quickly and easily? If you answered "yes" to the last three questions, then you are going to love Step #3 — "The Get Intuit Step." This step makes it easy for us to tap into our SIXTH SENSE, sometimes experienced as "knowing without knowing how we know." To be, do, and have all that you desire, you must go WITHIN, because this is where all answers and solutions reside. In other words, you must **go within** or **go without!**

Initially, you may have an issue with TRUSTING the answers you receive, or perhaps you are a bit concerned that you will receive answers you really DON'T WANT to HEAR. This is not uncommon. The only way that you will discover the value and validity of this step, however, is by just jumping in and DOING IT. Why not experiment with it and try it on for size? If it fits, do it again. If not, skip it and come back to it another time. Accessing answers is as easy as getting a glass of water. Just as water FLOWS into our glass when we turn on the faucet, answers FLOW into our awareness when we simply ASK QUESTIONS. Since the QUALITY of our questions determines the QUALITY of our lives, it behooves us to formulate them in ways that bring the most DESIRABLE RESULTS possible. The chart below is designed to help you STRUCTURE your questions in ways that benefit you most.

Instead of Asking...	Ask This Instead:
Why am I so sick?	What is the easiest way for me to regain my wellness?
What else can happen?	What can I do to regain my balance and move forward in life?
Why am I so miserable?	What is it that truly makes me happy?
Why am I always so tired?	What's the best way to naturally boost my energy?
What else could go wrong?	What can I do to get "back on track" in my life?
Why can't I find a good job?	How can I land a job that exceeds my wildest expectations?
Why can't I ever find the perfect mate?	How can I successfully attract the most ideal mate for me?
Why don't things ever work out for me?	How can I stay in the flow of Life, *regardless* of circumstances?
Why must I struggle to make ends meet?	What's the best way for me to generate abundant prosperity?
What if I make the wrong decision about...?	What do I need to know to make a wise decision about...?

Asking questions is like performing a SEARCH function on a computer. Each question causes you to tap into your "Storehouse of Infinite Wisdom" and display whatever you need to know on the "Monitor of Your Mind." Whatever comes up on your "Mental Screen" is coming from that part of you that KNOWS the answers you seek. Engaging in this step is a direct line to **IT** (your **In**Tuition, **I**nner **T**eacher, and/or **I**nvisible **T**herapist). If it is true that **In**Tuition is actually God speaking to you between your thoughts, you might want to really pay close attention to **IT**. If you really want to "get into **IT**," do "The Get Intuit Step!"

By asking well-structured questions, we invite an abundance of positive possibilities to permeate our lives. Since we have so many distracting thoughts racing through our minds each day, however, it is best to bring only ONE question at a time to the FOREFRONT of our awareness. As we gain valuable insights on ONE issue, we have a much better chance of resolving all of our OTHER issues. The more FOCUSED and CLEAR we are about what we want to know, the EASIER it is for Life to respond in ways we can clearly UNDERSTAND.

"But what if I receive answers I really don't want to hear?" you may ask. Well, here's GOOD NEWS: There's always a BENEFIT no matter what you decide to do! At the very least, you will gain greater experience from which to make WISER DECISIONS in the future. If you are feeling a bit STUCK and you need more ASSISTANCE in moving forward in your life, you will find great value in Step #4 (The Power Step). It invites you to SURRENDER all of your worries, doubts, and fears to a Higher Power that wisely guides your every step.

Mining for Joy in All the Right Places

Life is like a GOLD MINE, and I'm convinced I found the MOTHER LODE! What I am about to share has the potential to save you an entire lifetime of needlessly taking wrong turns that lead to dead ends. Before discovering The 15-Minute Miracle, I was constantly searching for ways to GET what I WANTED. After manifesting a multitude of things that I THOUGHT I wanted, I realized that the sense of personal fulfillment that I so longed to have was STILL just beyond my reach. This is when I began to make it my ONGOING INTENTION to find ways to be HAPPY under any and ALL circumstances. I began by simply asking the following question: **"How can I experience more contentment, peace, and joy?"** Here are the ANSWERS that immediately came into my awareness that made it possible for me to truly become "The HAPPIEST Person I Know."

- Instead of asking to always GET what you WANT…ask to WANT what you GET!
- Always express your HEARTFELT APPRECIATION for even the smallest of things.
- Make it your ongoing intention to see the MAGNIFICENCE in everyone you meet.
- Perceive each so-called CHALLENGE as a valuable OPPORTUNITY from which to learn.
- Make it your intention to see the BEAUTY and BENEFITS in everything you experience.
- Above all, find ways to enjoy WHATEVER you are doing WHENEVER you are doing it.

ONE POWER

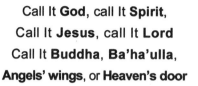

Words and Music by Daniel Nahmod

Call It **God**, call It **Spirit**,
Call It **Jesus**, call It **Lord**
Call It **Buddha**, **Ba'ha'ulla**,
Angels' wings, or **Heaven's door**

It's **Mohammed**, It's your **mind**,
It's your **soul** or It's your **sign**
It's the **Universe**, It's **music**,
Mother Earth or **Father Time**

It's the **moment of creation**,
It's an **everlasting peace**
It's the **freedom of forgiveness**,
It's the **sweetness of release**

It's the **joy of inspiration**,
It's the **sunshine on your face**
It's the **birthright of all nations**,
It's the **boundlessness of space**

It's the **beauty of a baby**,
The **serenity of sleep**
It's the **anger you abandon**,
for It's **LOVE that is most deep**

But whatever name you give It,
It's all **ONE POWER** can't you see
It's the **POWER of LOVE** in **YOU** and **ME**

To obtain a CD of this magnificent song, contact www.DanielNahmod.com or call 1-(888) 964-6683

Step #4

The ✳ Power Step

Prayer allows us to communicate with our **Higher Power;**
Intuition makes it possible for our Higher Power to communicate with **us.**

—Jacquelyn Aldana ✳ S.o.L.

I now invite ASSISTANCE from *The Loving Power* I recognize as greater than myself:

Thank You ____God____ for Your perfect guidance, unconditional love, and ongoing support. If it is in the highest good for me and for All Life Everywhere, please DIVINELY ORCHESTRATE the following in just the perfect time:

- Create perfect balance in ALL areas of my life.
- Guide me to be in the RIGHT place at the RIGHT time.
- Inspire our world leaders to advocate PEACE among ALL nations.

I completely SURRENDER all worries, doubts, and fears to You___God___. When I entrust YOU to take care of the details, everything falls into place for ME with amazing ease.

As you can readily see on the previous page, there are countless ways by which to address the infinite POWER we recognize as greater than ourselves. Although many refer to this Power as "God," we invite you to refer to YOUR Divine Connection with Life in a way that is most compatible with YOUR beliefs. This is a very PERSONAL thing and we totally respect this, because we honor ALL paths that lead to TRUTH.

Because this step invites assistance from a Higher Power that is considered SACRED, some people associate it with the "POWER of PRAYER," while others think it has more to do with the "POWER of THOUGHT." We are inclined to feel that BOTH concepts are equally correct. Many of our readers feel that this particular step is more powerful than ALL of the other steps combined, because it consistently summons a degree of pure positive energy that far EXCEEDS the limitations of our physical world. We suggest that you read an insightful book by Dr. Larry Dossey (a foremost authority on the power of prayer) called *Be Careful What You Pray For, You Just Might Get It.* It clearly explains WHY Step #4 is so valuable.

You're in good hands when
you fnally **surrender** all worries,
doubts, and fears to your Higher Power.

You had better hang on to your enthusiasm when you engage in THIS life-altering step, because it is absolutely INCREDIBLE what begins to happen when you ask Life for a HELPING HAND. At the very least, it allows you to become extremely CLEAR about what is most important to you. It is so comforting to be able to TRUST your Higher Power to divinely orchestrate the DETAILS of your life in ways that FREE you to attend to many other things. It is like hiring a talented STAFF of EXPERTS to do the job instead of having to do all the work YOURSELF. Ah-h-h-h! This is absolutely perfect for a LAZY MIRACLE WORKER like me!

"The Power Step" is very useful when dealing with those things we perceive to be beyond our own PERSONAL realm of influence. Since our Creator sees to it that the earth remains spinning on its axis and keeps the sun, the moon, and the stars in the sky day after day, it would be safe to assume that this Divine Presence is quite CAPABLE of orchestrating things of great magnitude! We are actually calling upon the very same energy that created our entire Universe whenever we ask for assistance from the ONE POWER described on page 86. OUR job is to be very CLEAR about our dreams and desires. LIFE'S job is to orchestrate the DETAILS and reveal Its ideal plan in just the PERFECT TIME. What could be easier than that?

Have you ever wondered why some prayers produce MIRACLES while others appear to go UNANSWERED? I can recall more than once thinking that my prayers were not even HEARD much less ANSWERED. I remember longing and yearning as I was begging and pleading with God to make it possible for us to buy a particular property that had a home on one semi-usable acre. I was absolutely DEVASTATED when someone else purchased it only five minutes before I even had a chance to show it to Ron. I figured that: 1) I was UNWORTHY of having what I wanted, 2) God never HEARD my prayer, or 3) God was PUNISHING me for something I did wrong. It never even occurred to me that The All-Knowing One had a much GRANDER plan for me until the following day when we became aware of a far more BEAUTIFUL home situated on three much-more-usable acres in an area that we liked far BETTER. Not only that, but the price was 25% LESS than the property I THOUGHT I wanted the day before! As it turns out, we purchased this cozy little horse ranch and have been living here for over 25 years. Thank God for what appear to be UNANSWERED PRAYERS. This provided a valuable LESSON that made quite an impression upon me. Ever since that day, I now pray to "WANT what I GET" instead of to "GET what I WANT!"

Ron and I look back on our lives and realize that even his challenging experience with cancer was a GIFT, because it led to the discovery of The 15-Minute → Miracle — a practical life management tool that is now helping thousands of people all over the world.

Are you familiar with the 99:1% theory? According to Buckminster Fuller, 99% of everything that most impacts our lives is invisible (things like thoughts, feelings, emotions, God, prayer, love, joy, imagination, oxygen, electricity, magnetism, gravity, airwaves, etc.). If this is true, it means that only 1% of everything in our world is perceptible through our PHYSICAL senses. By simply indulging in The 15-Minute → Miracle for just **1% of our day** (15 minutes), we can easily connect with that 99% of Life that enables us to tap into infinite power, knowledge, and wisdom. Being disconnected from 99% of our power is like trying to start a car with the battery disengaged. It is pretty hard to get to where we want to go in Life until we RECONNECT with our source of POWER. That's why "The Power Step" is so valuable. It allows us to CONNECT with our Divine Source through THOUGHT and PRAYER in ways that are as EASY as breathing, but a lot more FUN!

If you wish to visually SEE the power of prayer, visit www.earthtransitions.com and select the section entitled "Living Waters." On page 2 of this article, you will see the BEFORE AND AFTER photographs of molecules of water from a polluted lake at Fujiwara Dam in Japan. You will be amazed when you witness what happened after a Japanese priest prayed over this lake with the INTENTION of restoring it back to its natural state of purity.

This profound step begins with a sincere expression of APPRECIATION and gratitude. Next, we are invited to SPECIFY what we would like our Higher Power to orchestrate on our behalf. Then we get to completely SURRENDER all worries, doubts, and fears as we RELEASE our attachment to HOW and WHEN things happen. Once you see how powerful this step is, you'll realize what an enormous amount of ASSISTANCE is available to you whenever you CHOOSE to access it. Because the wording for this step (and all the other steps) was divinely inspired, it consistently invites the BEST possible results to occur at the BEST possible time for you. It also asks Life to reveal Its GRANDEST PLAN in delightful ways that express the highest good for All Life Everywhere. This way...

Everyone **benefits** and everyone **wins**!

Powerful ✳ Suggestions to Summon Divine Assistance

Thank You _God_ for your perfect guidance, unconditional love, and ongoing support. If it is in the **highest good** for me and for All Life Everywhere, please **divinely orchestrate** the following in just the **perfect time**:

- ♥ Inspire me to feel GRATEFUL for "what is" and EXCITED about "what is to come."
- ♥ Allow me to awaken fully REFRESHED each morning with joy and gratitude in my heart.
- ♥ Help me to RELEASE and let go of ANYTHING that no longer serves me in a positive way.
- ♥ Help me RELEASE all emotional BLOCKS, toxic THOUGHTS, and self-sabotaging BEHAVIOR.
- ♥ Make it easy for me to transform every CHALLENGE into a valuable OPPORTUNITY.
- ♥ Inspire me to love MYSELF unconditionally so I can love OTHERS in the same way.
- ♥ Help me to stay FULLY CONNECTED with my divine source of life-force energy.
- ♥ Reveal Your GRANDEST plan in ways that I can easily SEE and UNDERSTAND.
- ♥ Continue to remind me that I am WORTHY of health, happiness, and prosperity.
- ♥ Inspire me to see the BEAUTY and BENEFITS in ALL people and ALL situations.
- ♥ Inspire me to demonstrate IMPECCABLE INTEGRITY in all that I say and do.
- ♥ Provide whatever I need to demonstrate my HIGHEST PURPOSE for being.
- ♥ Show me ways to DO what I LOVE and to LOVE what I DO for a living.
- ♥ Inspire me to see the MAGNIFICENCE in even the SMALLEST of things.
- ♥ Allow me to perceive Life through the eyes of AWE and WONDER.
- ♥ Help me to BE the positive change that I want to SEE in the world.
- ♥ Help me to become the AWESOME person my dog thinks I am.
- ♥ Bless me with exceptional HEALTH in ALL aspects of my being.
- ♥ Show me delightful ways to enjoy EVERY step of my journey.
- ♥ Inspire me to live FULLY, love DEEPLY, and laugh OFTEN.
- ♥ Guide me to make WISE DECISIONS quickly and easily.
- ♥ Guide me to be in the RIGHT place at the RIGHT time.
- ♥ Create PERFECT BALANCE in ALL areas of my life.

⁎ Freedom

...a state of being that
naturally results from **releasing**
and **letting go** of all things both known
and unknown that no longer serve us
(or anyone else) in a positive way.

Step #5
The ✴ Freedom Step

To clear a perfect path to joy, to cherish every **minute**

Forgive yourself and all the world and everyone who's **in it**

Release, let go, and spread your wings and bask in all your **glory**

Now you know the choice is yours — now YOU create YOUR **story**!

—Jacquelyn Aldana ✴ S.o.L.

> **I am now READY and WILLING to RELEASE and LET GO of** all self-sabotaging PATTERNS and negative IMPRINTING
> **plus ALL ISSUES both known and unknown that no longer serve me in a positive way,**
> **which FREES me to** enjoy my Life and to accomplish my goals more EASILY.

In order to make room for the POSITIVE STUFF, we have to release and let go of the NEGATIVE STUFF. Likewise, to make room for the NEW STUFF, we must be willing to relinquish the OLD STUFF. In order to completely heal ANYTHING (including our physical bodies), we must be willing to RELEASE and let go of EVERYTHING that keeps us from LOVE, TRUTH, and SUSTAINED JOY. Although there may be several OTHER things you wish to release and let go of, in this chapter we are going to focus upon the things that seem to hinder us MOST. Because they fall into five major categories, we refer to them as **The BIG 5** — "The 5 Biggest Burdens" that keep us from our highest good.

This entire chapter is devoted to showing you very practical and productive ways to RENEW your spirit by releasing ANYTHING that no longer serves you (or anyone else) in a positive way. We invite you to FREE yourself from those walls of TOXIC THINKING that separate you from the PEACE and JOY that you deserve to have. Let's take a look at each one of **The BIG 5** and see if there are any benefits to holding on to them. If so, you are welcome to KEEP them. If not, you might want to RELEASE them. When you clear obstacles from your path, horizons expand and you can **"see far."** A very simple way to remember **The BIG 5** is to recall the letters **"C FARR"** (see explanation on pages 94-95).

Condemnation: To "condemn" is to negatively judge, blame, or criticize yourself or someone else for what is inappropriate or unacceptable by your standards. Although condemnation of others is certainly hazardous to your health, the most damaging form of condemnation is SELF-CONDEMNATION, because it makes it impossible for you to accept and appreciate yourself. Until you learn to love YOURSELF, it is hard for you to allow ANYONE ELSE to love you either. This makes it extremely difficult for you to experience close meaningful relationships. Since guilt doesn't serve you or anyone else in a constructive way, we suggest that you refer to the top of page 123 pertaining to FEELING GUILTY the next time you are tempted to punish yourself. With regard to condemning others, "Judge not that YE not be judged" is probably pretty good advice, because negative judgment is ALWAYS accompanied by negative consequences. Think about it! How do you feel when you BLAME, CRITICIZE, or CONDEMN someone else? If you are like most people, you probably feel LOUSY. How do these feelings benefit YOU? Since prolonged negative emotion COMPROMISES your health and well-being, why ALLOW it into you life?

Fear: I like to think of **FEAR** as just an acronym for "**F**orgetting **E**verything's **A**ll **R**ight." Fear is not always a bad thing, as it serves as a valuable ALARM that gets our attention so we can make wise decisions about the issues at hand. If, however, we allow fear to CHRONICALLY permeate our being, the results can severely hinder our ability to function in healthy, productive ways. When you attend our Level I Miracle ⇥⇤ Mastery Playshop or enroll in our "Positive Power of 3 Program," we teach you to master an amazing tool called **The One-Minute ⇥⇤ Miracle** that has often proven to bring IMMEDIATE comfort and peace of mind to even the most practiced worriers. It typically provides INSTANT RELIEF even for long-standing fears and phobias such as agoraphobia and panic attacks.

Attachments: Being attached to the outcome of things stems from the desire to CONTROL HOW and WHEN things happen. Because we CANNOT control events and the actions of other people, we find ourselves living in a state of ANXIETY doing everything we can to try to MAKE things happen. Being the lazy miracle worker that I am, I had to LET GO and allow The All-Knowing One to attend to the DETAILS of Life, because it was far too exhausting trying to do ALL of the work myself. If you truly wish to experience MIRACLES in YOUR life, get out of your own way long enough to allow Life's GRANDEST PLAN to be revealed to you. Perhaps you will become a lazy miracle worker TOO!

Resistance: Holding on to resistance is like driving down the highway of Life with your PARKING BRAKE on. Because the act of resisting requires the exertion of force to OPPOSE something, it subjects your body, mind, and spirit to enormous FATIGUE. Whenever I say, **"I have to...,"** I feel weak and tired. But when I say, **"I get to...,"** my energy kicks into high gear and I'm ready to leap tall buildings in a single bound! I no longer resist the CONTRAST of Life, because I've noticed that for every CHALLENGE that presents itself, there seems to be an equal or greater GIFT associated with it. Experience has taught me that when I choose to focus upon the CHALLENGE, all I see is the CHALLENGE. When I choose to look for the GIFT, I not only see it, but I am also GRATEFUL for the so-called challenge! Remember..."What we RESIST persists." Therefore, it is wise to RESIST NOTHING and EMBRACE EVERYTHING, because it ALL benefits us in some way.

Resentment: Hanging on to anger and resentment is like DRINKING POISON and expecting SOMEONE ELSE to die! Why hang on to something that has the power to eat you alive? That's about as wise as grabbing a CROCODILE by the tail! When you realize that "anything you have a hold of...also has a hold of YOU," you may choose to hang on to more positive things such as PEACE, FORGIVENESS, and COMPASSION instead!

The Big 5 are enormous burdens and can only drain us of our life-force energy until we make the decision to release them. Letting go of false beliefs and toxic emotions empowers us to experience much greater PEACE, POWER, and JOY in our lives. By embracing the PURIFYING POWER of LOVE, we automatically open our hearts. When we open our hearts, we also open the DOORS of OPPORTUNITY and the FLOODGATES of ABUNDANCE! Letting go of **C**ondemnation, **F**ear, **A**ttachment, **R**esistance, and **R**esentment is your ticket to FREEDOM. And freedom ranks right up there with OXYGEN when it comes to being "The Happiest Person You Know." Make it your intention to **"C FARR."**

When I let go of...	I feel...
Condemnation	much more compassionate and loving toward myself and others.
Fear (Anxiety)	secure in the belief that all is really well, REGARDLESS of appearances.
Attachments	confident that Life provides whatever serves me best in the perfect time.
Resistance	far more energetic, productive, and in harmony with Life.
Resentment	a lot lighter, freer, happier, and much better about myself.

Kindness

…a caring expression of **love**
and **compassion** for others that
brings out our highest nature and
greatly increases our sense of
value and self-worth.

Step #6

The ✳ Kindness Step

Expressing kindness to **others** causes us to fe-e-e-el good,
which is a perfect way to express kindness toward **ourselves**!

—Jacquelyn Aldana ✳ S.o.L.

My special way of being KIND to _____ someone else _____ **today is to** donate a full Miracle Discovery Program scholarship to Pat Gallagher (owner of The Book Café in Campbell, CA) for setting the all-time RECORD for selling MORE 15-Minute ✳ Miracle books in 2001 than any other bookstore in America (including Borders Books and Barnes & Noble)!

This step invites us to do something nice for SOMEONE ELSE, and it also lets us know that it's perfectly okay for US to have fun and be frivolous once in awhile. It invites Life to fill OUR cups, so we can more easily help others to fill THEIRS. This way, EVERYONE gets to have fun playing, and EVERYONE gets to win!

Be kind to yourself: Do something you LOVE to do — something that really makes your heart SING. When you set aside time each day to do something you really ENJOY, you honor ALL aspects of your being. This contributes greatly to your HEALTH, WELL-BEING, and PRODUCTIVITY. When YOU feel nurtured and cared for, you are inspired to be more nurturing and caring toward OTHERS.

Be kind to someone else: Expressing kindness for others has its OWN unique rewards. Nothing excites and delights me more than to imagine the immense JOY that another person might experience as a result of something I am able to contribute. As much as I enjoy RECEIVING gifts, I enjoy GIVING them even more. It absolutely THRILLS me to know that something I did or said added to the well-being of someone else!

Just as the light of the moon is **16 times stronger** than
the light of the stars, so loving kindness is **16 times more effective**
in liberating the heart than all religious accomplishments taken together.

—Buddha

97

✴ Tell-A-Vision

Tell me your **vision** and
I'll tell you your **future**! Clearly
envisioning Life the way you wish to
experience it invites your desires
to become REALIZED and your
dreams to come TRUE.

step #7
The "Tell-A-Vision" Step

"…All things for which you **pray and ask**,
believe that you have **already** received them,
and they shall be **granted** you."

—Mark 11:24

Since I can *be, do,* and *have* absolutely ANYTHING, I see myself ALREADY enjoying the following:

- I have plenty of TIME to indulge in the things I love to do!
- I am able to make a prosperous living doing something I ENJOY!
- My body is in better shape than it has EVER been in my entire life!

Have fun as you take an all-expense-paid "Creation Vacation" in your IMAGINATION. Allow your mind to playfully EXPLORE the positive possibilities of the future. The quickest way to attract miracles into your life is to see your dreams ALREADY REALIZED and your wishes ALREADY GRANTED. Bask in the feeling of APPRECIATION and CONTENTMENT as you create your perfect life in the playground of your imagination. This innovative step enables you to manifest things beyond your wildest expectations, because it invites you to build your dreams at "the speed of thought." Anything you can VISUALIZE in your imagination has the potential to become REAL in your life, so be sure to take ample time to HONOR your dreams and desires. Remember… "You have to have a DREAM to have a dream come TRUE."

Experiment with the fascinating principles of POSITIVE EXPECTANCY. Just believe in your heart that your wishes have ALREADY been granted (even though physical evidence may not yet be apparent). This is truly the most powerful ingredient in your recipe of deliberate creation, because it actually causes your SUBCONSCIOUS MIND to carry out your CONSCIOUS DESIRES. Just think — if you can successfully change the PROGRAMMING of your computer (your subconscious mind), you can successfully change the PRINTOUT of your life. What you can accomplish in just MINUTES, DAYS, or WEEKS with this step often takes SEVERAL YEARS of repeating affirmations to accomplish the same thing!

Just DECIDE what you want and CALL IT FORTH by reveling in how wonderful it would FE-E-E-EL to experience it. Focus only upon that which makes you SMILE, LAUGH, and feel FULLY CONNECTED with Life — those incredibly wonderful feelings that cause the floodgates of WELL-BEING to fly wide open for you!

Your job is to KNOW what you want. Life's job is to attend to all of the DETAILS (the who, when, why, where, and how). Therefore, just focus upon that which you DESIRE, then leave the rest to the discretion of the same magnificent Power that created all that is. Since you are very likely to GET whatever you ASK for, be sure to invite it to come to you in ways that are in HARMONY with your well-being. For instance, request that things come to you in just the PERFECT TIME and in ways that totally DELIGHT you. Otherwise, you may get what you want, but NOT in the appropriate time or in a way that is convenient. As Walt Disney often said to those who longed to turn their creative ideas into physical realities,

"If you can **dream it**, you can **do it**!"

Ron always tells me, "Life is just one big CANVAS — throw all the paint on it you can." The American billionaire, Donald Trump says, "Since you have to THINK anyway, you might as well think BIG!" Since you can be, do, and have absolutely ANYTHING your mind can conceive, what do you choose for yourself right NOW? What does your biggest DREAM look like? What do you choose to bring from your PAST that you want to carry FORWARD? Look at things as they CAN be — not limited to what they ARE right now. Visualization allows you to experience everything you desire in the PRIVACY of your own mind. Since ALL amazing manifestations BEGIN in the IMAGINATION, we recommend that you allow yourself to go there to play as often as you possibly can. According to Albert Einstein, the ultimate genius of the 20th century, "IMAGINATION is more important than KNOWLEDGE!"

Let's imagine for a moment that you are the director, producer, and STAR of your own television show. Tell me all about YOURSELF and what is going on in your life. By answering the questions on the next page, you can paint a colorful word picture to describe the life of your dreams. Create your DECLARATIONS to reflect what you DESIRE to experience as though it were ALREADY SO. By writing or speaking in the **first person/present tense**, you greatly amplify the effectiveness of this step. Use the examples on page 101 as your guide and you will find it very easy to create the NEW and IMPROVED "Story of Your Life."

Examples of Your Declarations

♥   I am by far "The HAPPIEST Person I Know."

♥   I enjoy multiple streams of RESIDUAL INCOME!

Based upon what you **DESIRE**, answer these questions in the FIRST person/PRESENT tense using COMPLETE sentences:

1. What is your overall state of being?

2. What degree of prosperity do you enjoy?

3. What are you currently doing vocationally?

4. What is the current status of your love life?

5. What are you most proud of and excited about?

6. What are you doing that is most rewarding for you?

7. What is your latest and greatest accomplishment?

8. How is your physical, mental, and emotional health?

9. What complimentary things are people saying about you?

10. What are you doing to contribute to the well-being of others?

CONGRATULATIONS! You are now an "Irresistible Magnet for Miracles!"

I absolutely LOVE "The Tell-A-Vision Step," because it allows me to create a sense of "Heaven on earth." By looking at reality through the lens of my IMAGINATION, troubles vanish, obstacles fall away, the lost become found, the sick become well, dark becomes light, and rough places become smooth. The imagination is the POWER we all possess in which we are able to see the HARMONY, UNITY, and BEAUTY in things. It's what links us to The Divine and brings into existence an indescribable sense of awe and wonder. Best of all, it enables us to see through "what APPEARS to be" to the positive possibilities of "what CAN be."

IMAGINATION is the most POWERFUL word in the dictionary.

It's the magic LAMP that lights up the mind. It banishes darkness.

It spotlights great ideas. It is the very HEART of creative thinking.

—Wilferd A. Peterson

Sacred Contract

…a contract to honor
all that is held sacred. Since
The 15-Minute ✳ Miracle is a
written agreement between you
and Life, it is definitely a
"sacred contract."

My  Sacred Contract

There is a difference between **wishing**
for something and being **willing** to **receive** it.

—Napoleon Hill

With enormous GRATITUDE, I now agree to ACCEPT these and even GREATER gifts in just the PERFECT TIME, in DELIGHTFUL WAYS that express the HIGHEST GOOD for All Life Everywhere!

Signed...✍_____ *Date*... _____

I am an "Irresistible Magnet for Miracles!" It's just the story of my life! MORE of this, please!
(Listen *as* Life whispers in your ear... **"You're RIGHT! Let me show you MORE EVIDENCE of this!"**)

One of the most important things for us to remember is that we can only RECEIVE as much as we BELIEVE we DESERVE. If we believe we deserve only a LITTLE goodness, Life will provide very LITTLE. Likewise, if we believe we are worthy of PROSPERITY, Life will respond by matching our beliefs with ABUNDANCE. What we experience is directly related to our belief about our WORTHINESS. This is why this segment of *The 15-Minute* ✳ *Miracle* is so important. It invites us to agree to ACCEPT the goodness that Life is so eager for us to have. A sense of worthiness is the FIRST STEP in becoming HAPPY and feeling FULFILLED.

Since *The 15-Minute* ✳ *Miracle* process offers only UNCONDITIONAL LOVE and UNIVERSAL ACCEPTANCE, it provides a comfortable bridge to SELF-LOVE and SELF-ACCEPTANCE. As it turns out, there's really only LOVE for you in this Universe. Since you have the freedom to CHOOSE, you can choose to ACCEPT IT or REJECT IT, but the fact still remains; LOVE is all there is!

In every moment we are **choosing**.
We're either winning or we're **losing**!

103

I Deserve to Be ⟩⟨ Happy

Those who feel they don't **deserve** hold their miracles in **reserve**!

—Michael Bisbiglia ⟩⟨ W.o.A. (Wizard of Ah-h-h-hs)

Before you embark upon your 15-Minute ⟩⟨ Miracle journey,
please read the following statements aloud and/or speak
them into a cassette recorder and play them back often.

I can only **RECEIVE** as much as I **BELIEVE** I **DESERVE**.
I now choose to believe that I **DESERVE** all that Life wants me to have!

I DESERVE to be happy, because it is Life's desire for me to experience joy.
When I am happy, I am a source of light and laughter to all those around me.

I am ENTITLED to be healthy, because it is Life's desire for me to be fit and strong.
When I am healthy, I serve as a positive role model for others who desire to thrive.

I am WORTHY of prosperity, because it is Life's desire for me to have unlimited abundance.
When I allow Life to fill my cup to overflowing, I am in a better position to help others fill theirs.

I DESERVE to have loving relationships, because it is Life's desire for me to love and be loved.
When I fall in love with Life and everything in it (including myself), I invite everyone else to do the same.

I DESERVE to take time out to nurture myself each day, because it is Life's desire for me to feel good.
When I take time out to do things that make my heart sing, I have more energy to be of greater value to others.

I DESERVE to do what I love and love what I do for a living, because it is Life's desire for me to feel fulfilled.
When I do what I love for a living, I express my highest purpose for being, while adding to the fulfillment of others.

Part 5

✵Thought

...an **idea**, **concept**, **intention**, or **belief**.
Thought is the **first cause** of every effect.
We actually BECOME what we **think** about through
the Law of Magnetic Attraction. We INVITE
every circumstance we experience through
the thoughts we CHOOSE to think.

What We ⟫⟪ Think About
Is What We ⟫⟪ Bring About

We either consciously or unconsciously INVITE every experience we have, based upon what we CHOOSE to think about, talk about, observe, imagine, or believe. **There are no exceptions** to this rule! If we CHOOSE to focus upon **problems**, our invitation might read as follows:

Attention All Problems and Negative Influences:

The Honor of Your Presence is Requested in the Life of

_____

Please come immediately, and bring along
all of your close relatives, namely:

Pain

Fear

Envy

Guilt

Anger

Stress

Illness

Anxiety

Resentment

Lack and Limitation

...and the rest of the gang.

This could very well be the **biggest pity party** you have attended all year!

Conversely, when we consciously CHOOSE to focus upon
solutions, our invitation is more likely to resemble this:

Attention All Solutions and Positive Aspects:

The Honor of Your Presence is Requested in the Life of

_____

I dearly love and appreciate each one of you. You are encouraged to
bring along all of your close friends, relatives, and associates, namely:

Joy

Love

Light

Peace

Beauty

Wisdom

Courage

Harmony

Happiness

Well-Being

Confidence

Prosperity

Abundance

Motivation

Inspiration

Perfect Health

☺ Please plan to stay forever, as there is only **love and appreciation** here for you. ☺

The Penetrating Power of Focus

Thoughts are extremely MAGNETIC and attract
whatever we choose to FOCUS our attention upon.
We will never ever **attract** the **Solution**
while we are **focused** upon the **Problem!**

We will **NEVER** attract...	while we are **FOCUSED** upon...
☺ LOVE	☹ RESENTMENT
☺ HAPPINESS	☹ SORROW
☺ HARMONY	☹ CONFLICT
☺ WELLNESS	☹ ILLNESS
☺ PEACE OF MIND	☹ ANXIETY
☺ ABUNDANCE	☹ SCARCITY
☺ SUCCESS	☹ FAILURE
☺ CONFIDENCE	☹ FEAR
☺ WELL-BEING	☹ WORRY
☺ PROSPERITY	☹ POVERTY
☺ COMPANIONSHIP	☹ LONELINESS

Although our THOUGHTS are very powerful, it is actually the FEELINGS behind our thoughts that enable us to successfully MANIFEST things (transform our wishes into realities). The power generated by our feelings accounts for the same kind of PHENOMENON that we experience when we hold a magnifying glass over a sheet of paper in direct sunlight. The sun generates so much energy (in the form of heat) that it can't help but result in SPONTANEOUS combustion — so it is with our thoughts and feelings. The MORE we focus upon a particular objective with FE-E-E-ELING, the MORE energy we attract to it. Our desire then becomes so amplified and expanded that it almost has no choice but to IGNITE into a physical reality!

I've been **rich**,
and I've been **poor**.
Rich is **better**!

—Mae West

Why the 😊 Rich Get Richer and the 🙁 Poor Get Poorer

Have you ever wondered why some people are very SUCCESSFUL in life in terms of loving relationships, good health, and prosperity, while others seem to have overwhelming CHALLENGES in one or more of these areas? Coming just a little closer to home…have you ever wondered why YOU sometimes feel absolutely INVINCIBLE, while at other times you feel like a HELPLESS VICTIM of circumstance?

To unravel this unsolved mystery, we must first know how we UNKNOWINGLY ATTRACT unwanted stuff into our lives in order to better understand how to CONSCIOUSLY ATTRACT what we PREFER instead. This single awareness will provide us with an invaluable gift more precious than all the gold in Fort Knox. When I first became aware of how I acquired MY so-called "lot in life," I was both SHOCKED and AMAZED! As you read the next paragraph, you may be taken aback at first, but when you read a little further you'll discover how YOU have the power to create a HAPPIER, more FULFILLING life in ways that are EASIER and more REWARDING than you have ever dreamed possible!

The shocking news is: WE are the creators of our OWN experience. WE are the ones who attract and create both what we DON'T WANT as well as what we DO WANT! Everything we experience is based upon what we CHOOSE to **think about, talk about, observe,** and **imagine.** What we **believe** also has an enormous influence over what prevails in our lives. Anything we say "yes" to, we automatically INVITE into our experience (ah yes). Likewise, whatever we say "no" to, we ALSO invite into our lives (oh-oh). In other words, whatever we CHOOSE to give our attention to (whether it's something wanted or unwanted) is what we are knowingly or unknowingly ASKING to become REAL in our lives. When you finally realize that "your energy FLOWS where your attention GOES," you will be highly motivated to keep your attention EXCLUSIVELY upon that which you DESIRE!

It's true! Our THOUGHTS have the POWER to create our realities — both good and bad, wanted and unwanted! We are certainly not implying that anyone INTENTIONALLY attracts and creates UNDESIRABLE experiences. For that matter, most of us are seldom aware of

111

how we attract POSITIVE circumstances into our lives. If we neglect to CONSCIOUSLY choose what we PREFER in life, we are doomed to live life by DEFAULT. Whatever we give our attention to is the very thing we can expect to call forth into being. Therefore, it is in our best interest to make it a habit to visualize the POSITIVE POSSIBILITIES of Life instead of dwelling upon things that WORRY us. If the state of "what is" doesn't appeal to you, then consciously SHIFT your attention and CLEARLY ENVISION "the life of your dreams." Above all, it is essential for you to imagine that your requests have ALREADY been granted. This is the golden KEY that opens the door to MIRACULOUS MANIFESTATIONS.

Since we can attract a quality of life that MATCHES the quality of our THOUGHTS, we can consciously create FAVORABLE conditions in our lives. We can use the power of our THOUGHTS, WORDS, FEELINGS, and IMAGINATION to intentionally improve the quality of our lives. This means we are NOT victims and that NOTHING can really hold power over us WITHOUT OUR CONSENT. It is so exciting to realize that most conditions in our lives are usually nothing more than expressions of our THOUGHTS, FEELINGS, and BELIEFS. Once again, whatever we THINK ABOUT and TALK ABOUT is what we are asking to BRING ABOUT!

So why is it that "the RICH get RICHER?" Perhaps it's because they have a tendency to focus upon PROSPERITY, and in doing so, they attract more ABUNDANCE. And why do "the POOR get POORER?" Maybe it's due to their overwhelming fear of SCARCITY, which causes them to stay focused upon POVERTY. Unfortunately, their limiting beliefs cause them to UNKNOWINGLY attract the very things they fear most, which results in even MORE LACK and LIMITATION in their lives. It helps to remember when we are feeling overwhelmed that **FEAR** is an acronym for "Forgetting Everything's **A**ll **R**ight" and that it's just temporary!

When we are POSITIVELY FOCUSED, we naturally attract an abundance of GOOD into our lives. When we are NEGATIVELY FOCUSED, however, we are more likely to see abundant evidence of LACK and LIMITATION. Both scenarios are perfect examples of the Law of Magnetic Attraction in action. Remember...this immutable universal law is ALWAYS at work. How you experience it is all based upon how you CHOOSE to focus your attention. Take time today to FOCUS upon things you DESIRE, such as: abundance, balance, health, happiness, harmony, peace, playfulness, prosperity, love, beauty, and sustained joy.

Now **notice** what you begin to magically **attract** and **create**!

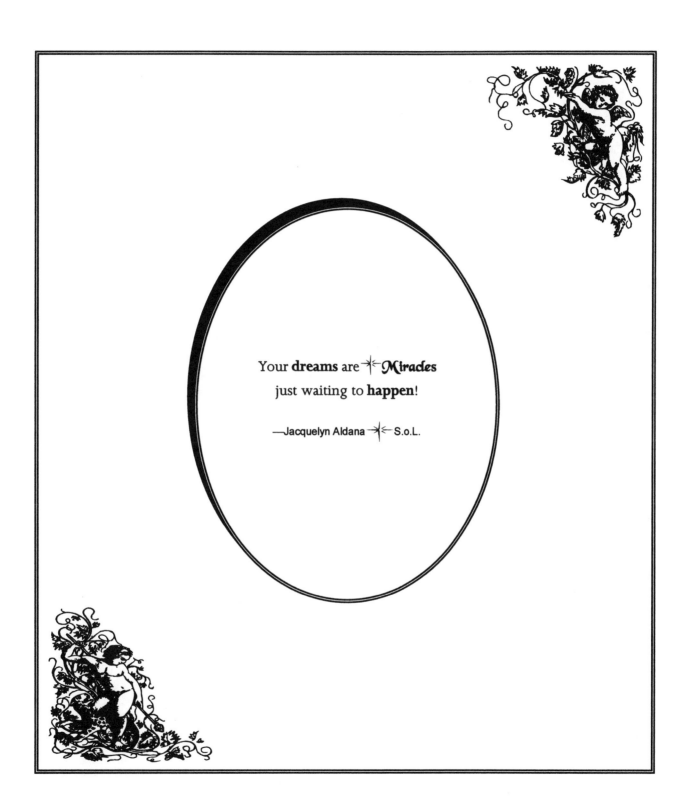

Your **dreams** are ✦ *Miracles*
just waiting to **happen**!

—Jacquelyn Aldana ✦ S.o.L.

Universal Laws

These are the immutable laws that apply to everyone in every moment with **no exceptions**! It is easy to experience a fulfilling life when we simply learn to work in **harmony** with them.

The 15-Minute ✳ Miracle™
How and Why It Works

We believe The 15-Minute ✳ Miracle works wonders for most anyone who engages in it, because it uses BABY STEPS to help us to RECONNECT with our INNATE WISDOM. It allows us to gracefully access the POWER, STRENGTH, and CREATIVITY that we ALREADY HAVE, thereby making it possible for us to feel GOOD, have FUN, and achieve our GOALS more easily! Whoever would have thought that personal fulfillment could be as easy as writing a "Love Letter to Life?"

This user-friendly technique works so consistently because it is based upon ageless wisdom and universal laws that are ABSOLUTE. These laws operate EVERY moment of EVERY day and they work exactly the SAME for each of us. There are NO exceptions! By simply learning to work in HARMONY with them, we possess everything we need to enhance the quality of our lives beyond our wildest expectations. Below is a brief explanation of the unchangeable laws and principles that we consider most important for you to understand.

The Law of Magnetic Attraction — this powerful law says, "What we THINK ABOUT is what we BRING ABOUT." It also says, "What we FILL our minds with, our lives are FULL of." Our thoughts are truly MAGNETIC, which means that they draw people, places, and circumstances into our lives that MATCH the focus of our attention. A thought irresistibly attracts all other thoughts and conditions that are in HARMONY with it — just like a piece of magnetite (magnetic iron ore) naturally attracts iron. This is why I now consciously CHOOSE to dwell upon the POSITIVE aspects of Life. When I focus upon things that I LOVE and APPRECIATE, I not only feel wonderful, but my entire life reflects a POSITIVE outcome. When I focus upon things that WORRY or annoy me, I not only feel LOUSY, but I also inadvertently attract even MORE annoying things that cause me to worry and fret. Now that I realize how this law works, I pay very close attention to what I THINK ABOUT and TALK ABOUT!

The Law of Inclusion — this law says, "We automatically INCLUDE into our life everything we CHOOSE to think about, talk about, observe, and imagine." Just as things we say "yes" to are automatically INCLUDED, things we say "no" to are INCLUDED as well! I envision myself in the "imaginary supermarket of Life" with a huge magnetic shopping cart that NON-SELECTIVELY attracts everything I give my attention to. Now that I realize that EVERYTHING I focus upon (both wanted and unwanted) goes into my cart, I consciously CHOOSE to stay focused ONLY upon what I DO WANT!

The Law of Cause and Effect — this law says, "What GOES around COMES around" or "Whatever we do FOR others, we also do FOR ourselves." Likewise, "Whatever we do TO others, we also do TO ourselves." This law is the ultimate expression of The Golden Rule that says, "Do unto OTHERS as you would have others do unto YOU." The awareness of it inspires me to regard All Life Everywhere with abundant LOVE, APPRECIATION, and RESPECT, because I prefer to experience these same qualities in my OWN life. In short, this law says, "**I am the CAUSE of my EFFECT!**"

The Law of Positive Expectancy — this law says, "What we EXPECT is what we GET!" This is why Ron and I choose to expect the very BEST that Life has to offer. Life seems to readily AGREE with whatever we say and provides EVIDENCE of whatever we EXPECT to happen. For instance, when I say, "I KNOW I will SUCCEED." Life responds by saying, "You're RIGHT, Jacquelyn! Let me show you MORE EVIDENCE of that!" Likewise, when I say, "I just KNOW I am going to FAIL." Life responds by saying, "You're RIGHT, Jacquelyn! Let me show you MORE EVIDENCE of that!" If you prefer to enjoy more ease, joy, and comfort in your life, you might want to make a habit of asking yourself the following question: "What do I want to be RIGHT about TODAY?"

The Law of Allowing — this law says, "I AM that which I AM and I ALLOW all others to BE that which they ARE." This statement essentially means "LIVE and LET live." or "Judge not that YE not be judged." Once I finally released and let go of the habit of judging and criticizing MYSELF and OTHERS, I noticed that OTHERS were less inclined to judge and criticize ME. I guess I must have had a "judgectomy" without even realizing it, and I am sure glad I did! It causes me to OPEN my heart and CLOSE my mouth every time I am tempted to criticize or condemn MYSELF or someone ELSE.

The Law of Surrender — this law says, "SURRENDER your worries, doubts, and fears to your Higher Power and RELEASE YOUR ATTACHMENT to the outcome of things." This is often our greatest challenge, because most of us desire to CONTROL how and when things happen. When we feel "out of control," we usually feel anxious and fearful that things won't work out to our satisfaction. In the moment we allow anxiety and fear to dominate our thoughts, we unknowingly "set it up" to experience the very things we DON'T WANT — lack, limitation, and failure. One of the most comfortable ways I have found to let go of any attachments is to ask Life to provide things in just the **perfect time** and in **delightful ways** that express the **highest good** for All Life Everywhere!

The Law of The 15-Minute ⨯ Miracle — Whereas the Law of Gravity says, "What goes UP must come DOWN," this law says, "What goes DOWN must come UP!" It also implies that if a PHYSICAL FACT can produce a PSYCHOLOGICAL STATE, then a PSYCHOLOGICAL STATE can produce a PHYSICAL FACT. This law is especially valuable when it comes to regaining our balance and sense of well-being. Ron and I firmly believe that this law played a major part in his ability to regain his wellness. When Ron's disease (a negative physical fact) produced ANXIETY and FEAR (a negative psychological state), he consciously focused upon GRATITUDE and LOVE (a positive psychological state), which produced RADIANT HEALTH (a positive physical fact). The MORE he appreciated every moment he had left to live, the MORE time he was given to experience Life. In 1991, his doctors gave him very little hope. Today, (12 years later) he is STILL ALIVE and THRIVING (thank You, God)!

The universal laws that govern the quality of our lives are ALWAYS at work. The way in which they affect our lives, however, is entirely up to US. It really matters not that we UNDERSTAND them or even BELIEVE in them. Just like the Law of Gravity, they work REGARDLESS of all that. The wisest thing to do is to figure out how to work in HARMONY with these laws. By faithfully practicing The 15-Minute ⨯ Miracle, you are automatically guided to work in accordance with all of the above universal laws in ways that will serve you extremely well. We believe that by MASTERING The 15-Minute ⨯ Miracle, you will also MASTER your ability to become…

"The **Happiest** Person You Know" and "An **Irresistible** Magnet for Miracles!"

To gain the GREATEST BENEFIT from practicing your 15-Minute ☀ Miracle, make a point to NOTICE how you fe-e-e-e-el at all times. When you feel a sense of COMFORT, you are "in the flow of Life." When you feel a sense of DISCOMFORT, you are temporarily "disconnected" from your Power Source. All you need to do to get BACK ON TRACK is to find something (anything) to APPRECIATE, or simply give your attention to something that makes you FEEL GOOD just to THINK about it. When you do this on a regular basis, you will definitely experience a greater sense of JOY and deeper sense of WELL-BEING.

Every THOUGHT we have greatly affects our health and physical well-being. When we think POSITIVE THOUGHTS, our bodies absolutely THRIVE. Our magnificent internal pharmacy magically produces a multitude of wonderful immune-boosting chemicals and hormones such as interferon, interleukins, and endorphins. These substances are natural drugs produced by our own bodies. They possess powerful health-enhancing properties that automatically SUPERCHARGE our immune systems. In fact, endorphins are one of nature's most efficient ANALGESICS. They effectively relieve physical pain because (according to scientific studies) they are **four times more potent than morphine**. We suggest you read *Anatomy of an Illness* by Norman Cousins to better understand the amazing healing power of POSITIVE THINKING and LAUGHTER. Norman literally laughed himself well!

When we think NEGATIVE THOUGHTS related to worry, fear, anger, resentment, etc., our bodies produce toxic chemicals that greatly SUPPRESS our immune systems. Dr. Deepak Chopra, a well-known author and endocrinologist, claims that our blood can actually become LETHAL when we experience strong negative emotions. It has been scientifically proven that just a couple of drops of this deadly blood injected into a healthy hamster can KILL it immediately! In fact, a mother experiencing extreme negative emotions unavoidably passes harmful chemicals into her breast milk, which can seriously jeopardize the health of her nursing baby. Just imagine how we are poisoning our bodies with our prolonged TOXIC THINKING. This explains why we usually get SICK when we are LEAST happy about life. Have you noticed how tired and lethargic you become when things aren't going your way?

As a result of my own personal experience, I have come to the conclusion that the BODY is literally a SLAVE to the MIND. In fact, Barbara H. Levine wrote a book about this entitled *The Body Believes Every Word You Say*. There is also an amazing phenomenon with

118

regard to **MPD** (**M**ultiple **P**ersonality **D**isorder). There have been documented studies showing unexplainable changes in body chemistries when patients switch from one personality to another. For example, someone with a long-standing history of SEVERE ALLERGIES may have NO ALLERGIC REACTION when changing personalities. Patients with MALIGNANT TUMORS as one personality may have NO EVIDENCE OF CANCER whatsoever when switching to an alternate personality. Had this not been MEDICALLY DOCUMENTED, it would probably be somewhat difficult to believe! It just shows us how powerful our MINDS are with respect to our PHYSICAL BODIES.

When you are CONFIDENT and HAPPY, you are better able to see the POSITIVE aspects of Life. As you focus upon the goodness of Life, GOODNESS becomes your personal "Point of Attraction." Whatever thoughts and feelings you allow to DOMINATE your attention is what you can expect to ATTRACT and EXPERIENCE. As it turns out, you have a great deal of INFLUENCE over your personal destiny. You are far more powerful than you probably realize. As Napoleon Hill said in his wonderful book *Think and Grow Rich*, "Whatever the mind of man can CONCEIVE and BELIEVE, he can ACHIEVE." When we clearly envision ourselves as CONFIDENT, CAPABLE, and ACCOMPLISHED, we automatically create the perfect conditions for MIRACLES to occur in our lives. It's really exciting to realize that...

We can **redirect our lives** by simply **redirecting our thoughts**!

It is not absolutely essential that you even understand how The 15-Minute Miracle works in order to BENEFIT from it. It's sort of like electricity — the average person cannot explain exactly HOW it works, but they agree that it DOES work and that they DO use it. So it is with The 15-Minute Miracle. If you practice it regularly with PURE INTENTIONS and remain POSITIVELY FOCUSED, it is bound to work WONDERS in your life.

✳ Antidote

...a remedy that **relieves**,
prevents, or **counteracts**
the effects of poison.

Positive —✳← Antidotes to Negative Thinking

Arnold Patent wrote a book entitled *If You **Know** What You **Want** You Can **Have** It*. This is a great book title, but what if you DON'T KNOW what you want? Over the past seven years, Ron and I have discovered that it is sometimes easier for us to discern what we DO WANT by briefly (and I mean briefly) contemplating what we DON'T WANT. On the pages that follow, you will find a variety of examples to give you ideas of how to easily COUNTER your NEGATIVE FEELINGS with empowering POSITIVE THOUGHTS that enable you to magnetize MIRACLES into your life. When you learn to MIRACLE-IZE your thoughts, you can MIRACLE-IZE your destiny!

Notice how BRIEF the **Negative Statements of Contrast** are compared to the **Positive Statements of Desire**. The LESS time you spend focusing upon what you DON'T WANT, and the MORE time you spend envisioning what you DO WANT, the more successful you will be at consciously attracting and creating what you PREFER. This is why each Statement of Contrast is extremely SHORT and every Statement of Desire is a bit LENGTHY. We have found that by staying totally FOCUSED upon a positive idea for at least 15-30 SECONDS, we increase our odds of success SUBSTANTIALLY. The example below is an excellent illustration of this philosophy. The rest of the examples are helpful in inviting your OWN creative juices to flow. Refer to these statements whenever you need a little EMOTIONAL JUMPSTART.

Example

Resistance ♥ If I am thinking, **"I really dread getting up in the morning."** I simply write:

"It's fun to feel a strong sense of POSITIVE ANTICIPATION about Life when I wake up in the morning. When I look FORWARD to my day with ENTHUSIASM, a tremendous surge of ENERGY wells up within me, which makes it easy for me to ACCOMPLISH all that I set out to do. Today, **I AM** an expression of OPTIMISM as I cheerfully awaken to the POSITIVE POSSIBILITIES that abound!"

Several of our favorite Statements of Desire that have proven to work extremely well begin on the next page. YOUR best results will come from using words that evoke strong, positive feelings within YOU. Your creative ideas serve to attract MORE of whatever you focus upon. The **"I AM"** statements definitely add an affirmative punch to your declarations. In fact, we recommend that you HIGHLIGHT them with a magic marker and refer to them often.

Confrontations ♥ If I am thinking, **"I dread having confrontations with _____."** I simply write:

"I now consciously choose to invite harmony, warmth, and understanding into my relationship with _____. As I take the time to APPRECIATE his (her) positive qualities, I automatically begin to feel better, and he (she) seems to respond to ME in a much more positive way as well. This, in turn, allows me to feel much more encouraged, uplifted, and VALIDATED. As I release MY need to judge and control the actions of OTHERS, others are then inspired to release THEIR need to judge and control ME. Releasing and letting go of condemnation is one of the most freeing and empowering things I have ever experienced. Today, **I AM** totally FREE and extremely RELIEVED as I release the temptation to judge and control _____."

Confusion ♥ If I am thinking, **"I just don't know what I want."** I simply write:

"I now choose to discover what really warms my HEART and fans the fire in my SOUL. When I have a CLEAR PICTURE of what I truly desire to BE, DO, and HAVE, I can EASILY attract it into my life. It's fun to focus upon my DREAMS until they magically IGNITE into physical REALITIES. I feel so blessed to be able to consciously attract and create whatever my heart desires through the power of my INTENTION. The best part is that it is all so EASY. Today, **I AM** an expression of POSITIVE ANTICIPATION as I eagerly look forward to the magnificent unfolding of LIFE'S GRANDEST PLAN!"

Depression ♥ If I am thinking, **"I am tired of feeling so depressed."** I simply write:

"I consciously choose to align myself with feelings of CONTENTMENT, EASE, and JOY from this day forward. When I embrace these feelings, I experience abundant ENERGY and ENTHUSIASM, which empowers me to be, do, and have whatever makes my heart sing. I love that inexplicable feeling of being FULLY CONNECTED with Life, because it reminds me that I have a multitude of POSITIVE POSSIBILITIES from which to choose. The quickest way for me to RECONNECT with Life and to feel GOOD is to find people and/or things to APPRECIATE and ADMIRE. I also feel INSPIRED and ENCOURAGED when I merely RECALL the many things for which I am GRATEFUL. Today, **I AM** a magnificent expression of PRAISE, APPLAUSE, and APPRECIATION. I am so blessed!"

Guilt ♥ If I am thinking, **"I feel so guilty about** _____**."** I simply write:

"I now choose to invite a sense of self-acceptance and INNER PEACE into my life that allows me to realize that I am STILL a good person even when I make mistakes from time to time. Although I sometimes make decisions that I later regret, I always LEARN from every experience, which enables me to make much WISER decisions next time. Today, **I AM** an expression of impeccable INTEGRITY as I invite my Higher Power to wisely guide my every step, inspiring me to be kind, compassionate, and understanding of OTHERS in every moment. I also remember to extend this SAME degree of kindness, compassion, and understanding to MYSELF!"

Frustration ♥ If I am thinking, **"I can't seem to do much of anything right."** I simply write:

"It is so empowering to feel a genuine sense of self-appreciation and self-confidence. When I feel LOVABLE and CAPABLE, I feel GOOD about myself, which causes an abundance of positive people and experiences to be drawn into my life in ways that amaze and delight me. I now choose to RELEASE and let go of all things (both known and unknown) that no longer serve me in a positive way. Today, **I AM** an enlightened expression of self-realization as I fondly remember the POSITIVE things that OTHERS have said about me in the past."

Illness ♥ If I am thinking, **"I am sick and tired of feeling so sick and tired."** I simply write:

"I now choose to discover an easy way by which to enjoy RADIANT HEALTH from now on. I love being able to naturally exude ABUNDANT ENERGY. When I feel mentally SHARP and physically STRONG, I perceive Life with extraordinary OPTIMISM, which automatically attracts MORE things for which to be grateful. As I find additional things to appreciate, I feel better and I enjoy even MORE energy. Today, **I AM** a radiant expression of WELLNESS as I acknowledge and appreciate my resilient body that operates with AMAZING PRECISION."

Insomnia ♥ If I am thinking, **"If only I could fall asleep at night."** I simply write:

"I am so fortunate to be able to completely RELAX when I lie down to rest. It feels so good to be able to DRIFT OFF naturally into a deep, peaceful SLEEP whenever I choose to. It is wonderful to have such PLEASANT DREAMS and wake up feeling totally REFRESHED in the morning. When I enjoy a good night's sleep, I am naturally inspired to appreciate Life, which enables me to enjoy my day even MORE. Today, **I AM** completely RENEWED as I recall times in the past when I fell asleep as easily and naturally as a NEWBORN BABY."

Loneliness ♥ If I am thinking, **"I sure wish I had someone special in my life."** I simply write:

"I now choose to extend a warm invitation to my IDEAL MATE to come into my life in just the PERFECT TIME in ways that totally delight me. I love the kind of relationship that allows us to bring out the BEST in one another. My primary intention is to attract a thoughtful and gentle person with a fabulous sense of humor who is easy to get along with and enchanting to be with. I look forward to experiencing the magic of a SPECIAL CONNECTION that is so harmonious that words cannot even BEGIN to describe how wonderful it feels. When I merely ponder this "perfect partnership," I experience a wonderful sense of WELL-BEING and positive anticipation about Life, which enables me to easily express all of the same qualities that I am seeking in my mate. Today, **I AM** a loving expression of JOY, EXHILARATION, and SPONTANEITY as I offer my heart to my BEST FRIEND and my FUTURE PARTNER."

Pain ♥ If I am thinking, **"If only I could get rid of this pain in my body."** I simply write:

"I love it when I feel COMFORTABLE and FLEXIBLE in my body. Just CONTEMPLATING this state of being BOOSTS my energy. As my body naturally regains its BALANCE, I am inspired to make the MOST of every precious moment; therefore I am willing to settle for NOTHING LESS than RADIANT HEALTH from now on. Since countless OTHERS have successfully regained their wellness, I know that I can do it TOO! I am blessed with an exceptionally STRONG CONSTITUTION and my body heals very QUICKLY. Today, **I AM** a joyous expression of GRATITUDE as I give thanks for ALL of the aspects of my physical body that continue to serve me well. I appreciate the degree of comfort that I ALREADY ENJOY and look forward to even MORE vitality with each day that passes."

Poverty ♥ If I am thinking, **"I hate struggling to just make ends meet."** I simply write:

"I now choose to find easy and interesting ways to create ABUNDANT WEALTH. Just as I KNOW that I have access to plenty of air to breathe, water to drink, and thoughts to think, I also KNOW that I can claim as much HAPPINESS and PROSPERITY as I am WILLING to ACCEPT for myself. When I allow Life to fill my cup to OVERFLOWING, I am then able to share my good fortune with others. This empowers me to be of greater value to MYSELF and everyone ELSE. Today, **I AM** a stellar expression of AFFLUENCE, because I am now willing to graciously ACCEPT my Divine Inheritance. Starting today, I am completely open to RECEIVE SURPRISE GIFTS and UNEXPECTED INCOME from positive sources I have yet to discover."

Procrastination ♥ If I am thinking, **"I'll deal with that when I have more time."** I simply write:

"I now choose to find simple and creative ways to accomplish things that (up until now) I have had great RESISTANCE to even starting. I "WANT to WANT" to start and FINISH my projects in ways that are FUN, INTERESTING, and ENTERTAINING. When I accomplish what I set out to do, I feel EXTREMELY GOOD about myself. The positive momentum naturally PROPELS me to accomplish even MORE. I especially appreciate the wonderful PEACE OF MIND that I experience when there is ORDER in my life. Today, **I AM** an outstanding expression of ACHIEVEMENT as I discover the QUICKEST and most ENJOYABLE ways by which to meet or EXCEED my personal goals."

Vocation ♥ If I am thinking, **"I'm out of work and I can't find a decent job."** I simply write:

"I now choose to tap into the state of awareness that allows me to easily recognize my perfect VOCATIONAL OPPORTUNITY. When I avail myself to all POSITIVE POSSIBILITIES, I am often surprised as incredible situations just MAGICALLY unfold. I look forward to finding my IDEAL JOB in just the PERFECT TIME in ways that invite my confidence to SOAR. This encourages me to stay focused upon an exciting NEW ADVENTURE that I have yet to discover. Today, **I AM** a pure positive expression of enthusiasm, because I KNOW there are several outstanding employers actively looking for someone with MY skills, experience, and integrity. In fact, they are probably actively searching for me RIGHT NOW!"

Worry ♥ If I am thinking, **"I wish I didn't worry so much about everything."** I simply write:

"I now choose to invite a sense of well-being and a strong inner knowing that I am EQUAL to any challenge that Life may offer me for the purpose of EXPANDING my awareness. When I am consciously AWARE of things, I approach Life from a more POSITIVE perspective, which empowers me to attract desired results easily and effortlessly. It is so good to feel IN CHARGE of my life. Today, **I AM** a glowing reflection of WELL-BEING as I acknowledge the abundant evidence that Life is GOOD and all is WELL." Remember…

Energy **flows** where your attention **goes**,
so focus **exclusively** upon your **Statements of Desire!**

Love is my form,
Truth is my breath,
and bliss is my food.
My life is my message.

—Si Baba

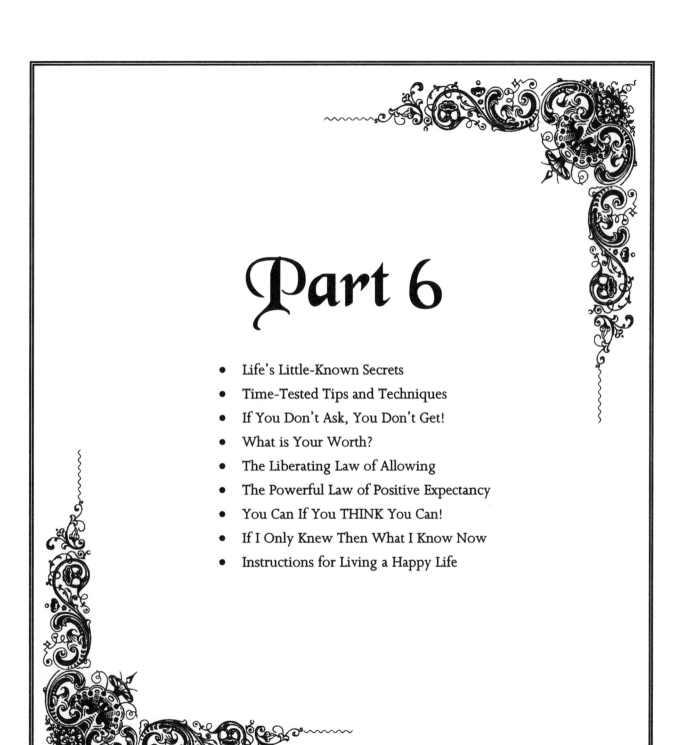

Part 6

- Life's Little-Known Secrets
- Time-Tested Tips and Techniques
- If You Don't Ask, You Don't Get!
- What is Your Worth?
- The Liberating Law of Allowing
- The Powerful Law of Positive Expectancy
- You Can If You THINK You Can!
- If I Only Knew Then What I Know Now
- Instructions for Living a Happy Life

✳ Secrets

...knowledge lying **beyond**
ordinary comprehension and
known only by very **few**.

Life's ✳ Little-Known Secrets

How to Succeed Against All Odds

When the DREAM is BIG enough, FACTS don't matter! This reminds me of the famous BUMBLEBEE theory. A group of esteemed scientists got together and proved beyond a shadow of a doubt that it is aerodynamically IMPOSSIBLE for bumblebees to fly, but apparently no one informed the bumblebee! I remember when doctors told Ron, based upon their decades of experience, that he might have only a FEW MONTHS left to live. At that point Ron said, "If ANYONE has ever overcome cancer, then I can do it TOO. Even if NO ONE has ever done it, then I shall be the FIRST!" I then said to Ron, "Although I don't know exactly HOW you will fully regain your wellness, I DO know that we will DEFINITELY find a way!" Both of these heartfelt statements are what we refer to as **DOC's** (Declarations **Of** Commitment). Ron and I have found them to be EXTREMELY POWERFUL. Once we "called in the **DOC's**" then ANSWERS, SOLUTIONS, and POSITIVE POSSIBILITIES began to flow in from everywhere. Once we made the FIRM COMMITMENT to succeed (even before we had any clue as to HOW that was even possible), Life orchestrated the details and delivered the BEST POSSIBLE RESULTS in just the PERFECT TIME in ways that totally amazed everyone.

How to Regain Your Health Naturally

Because the degree of our HEALTH is a reflection of the quality of our THOUGHTS, we find that we have the BEST chance of experiencing radiant health when we stay focused EXCLUSIVELY upon WELLNESS. When we dwell upon ILLNESS, MISERY, and PAIN, we unavoidably attract MORE of the same. Likewise, when we envision ourselves as STRONG, ENERGETIC, and HEALTHY, we begin to attract whatever is needed to MATCH this glowing picture of health. Another essential key to greatly enhancing our health is to CONSCIOUSLY ACKNOWLEDGE and APPRECIATE all aspects of our bodies that ARE working. Since Life loves to bring MORE of whatever we admire, praise, and appreciate, we are likely to enjoy SECOND HELPINGS of comfort, ease, and joy when we express GRATITUDE for our blessings. Next, create your **D**eclaration **Of** Commitment (see reference to **DOC's** in the preceding paragraph), as this is the MAGIC INGREDIENT in the recipe of health and well-being.

How to Overcome Common Feelings of Unworthiness

So many of us, on a very deep level, believe that we really DON'T DESERVE very much, and therefore we find it difficult to ACCEPT the riches that Life wants us to have. Since we can only RECEIVE as much as we BELIEVE we DESERVE, it is essential that we find ways to feel deserving of health, wealth, and happiness. Until we love and accept OURSELVES, we are not likely to allow OTHERS to love and accept us either. A quick and simple way to BOOST your self-esteem is to create a COMPLIMENT COLLECTION and write down every NICE thing that anyone has ever said about you. Make it a daily practice to ADD to this collection at every opportunity and also make a list of all of the traits and characteristics that YOU like about you. Since we teach OTHERS how to treat us by the way we treat OURSELVES, it behooves us to treat ourselves with a healthy dose of LOVE and RESPECT. When we simply remember that WE are the offspring of the same LOVING POWER that created us, we can more easily claim our DIVINE HERITAGE and begin to open our hearts to receive all the infinite goodness of Life. If you want to be able to GIVE to others, you must first be willing to RECEIVE. Just remember…the more you HAVE, the more you HAVE to GIVE. Read and reread the section on page 104 entitled **"I Deserve to be Happy."** Also read **"Instructions for Living a Happy Life"** (starting on page 154) until you realize that YOU are an ESSENTIAL PIECE in the puzzle of Life. Without YOU, LIFE is incomplete. YOU truly matter because YOU, Magnificent One, are a Perfect and Divine Expression of The Creator of All That Is!

How to Enjoy More Harmony in Your Relationships

According to Dr. Candice Pert, the author of *Your Body is Your Subconscious Mind*, humans are hard-wired to desire CLOSE RELATIONSHIPS with others. If this is true, it seems it would definitely be to our advantage to know how to enjoy consistent HARMONY in these relationships. In a nutshell, the most comfortable way to accomplish this is to make it your ONGOING INTENTION to see the MAGNIFICENCE in each and every person you meet. Stay focused upon their ADMIRABLE QUALITIES and tell them what you like MOST about them. Also be willing to ALLOW OTHERS to acknowledge YOUR positive aspects as well. If you apply the simple principles on "How to Become the Most Popular Person on the Planet" (page 133), you are bound to win TOP AWARDS in the relationship department!

How to Become More Prosperous

Here are 7 EASY-TO-DO things that have repeatedly PROVEN to generate amazing amounts of UNEXPECTED INCOME among those who have experimented with these ideas:

1) Start by writing down EVERYTHING that you have ever heard, read, or said about money, wealth, and prosperity. Write the NEGATIVE and POSITIVE statements on separate sheets of paper so you can later BURN the statements, declarations, and beliefs that no longer serve you in a positive way. This has proven to greatly impact the mind in a LASTING, POSITIVE WAY. Be sure to keep the pages of POSITIVE comments and continue to ADD to them as new ideas come into your awareness.

2) Next, ask yourself the following question: "Do I DESERVE to be wealthy?" If the answer is anything other than "yes," review the instructions on **"How to Overcome Feelings of Unworthiness"** on the previous page. As long as you feel UNDESERVING of prosperity, Life will CONTINUE to keep abundance just beyond your r-e-a-c-h!

3) Make a list of three people whom you RESPECT that are as prosperous as YOU aspire to be. These can be HEROES from history, famous CELEBRITIES, or people you know PERSONALLY. Make a note of all their positive traits, then CLAIM these characteristics for YOURSELF. You must have at least ONE prosperous role model that you truly admire before you are likely to transform your WISHES into REALITIES.

4) Determine the approximate AMOUNT of money you will need to MATCH your desires and write down how you plan to SPEND, INVEST, and otherwise ENJOY your wealth.

5) Now it's time to express SINCERE APPRECIATION for the prosperity you ALREADY HAVE. Remember...Life loves to bring MORE of what you LOVE and APPRECIATE.

6) Another important part of this process is to write your STATEMENT of ACCEPTANCE and read it aloud in front of the mirror when you first wake up in the MORNING and every NIGHT just before you go to sleep. In other words, "Read 'em and reap!"

7) Wise farmers who RETURN 10% of their crops to the soil seem to enjoy a HIGHER YIELD from future crops. Interestingly, people who GIVE BACK a portion of whatever Life gives to them seem to consistently enjoy a HIGHER YIELD of joy and prosperity.

How to Overcome Anxiety, Fears, and Phobias

Most of us experience varying degrees of FEAR and ANXIETY from time to time, but we usually manage to function in spite of all this. When, however, we experience physical symptoms like dizziness, dry mouth, blurry vision, hyperventilation, racing heart, chest pains, and/or sweaty palms, we may be experiencing a little-understood condition called PANIC DISORDER (more commonly known as PANIC ATTACKS). This enslaving condition causes people to feel totally HOPELESS and HELPLESS to do even SIMPLE things that others can do without so much as a second thought — things like leaving the house, standing in line in public places, dining in restaurants, going shopping, driving a car, etc.

If any of these things sound remotely familiar, you'll be glad to know that there is something that has PROVEN to work wonders for many who suffer from this disorienting condition. It is a simple MERIDIAN-BASED healing technique that you can do WITH YOURSELF and BY YOURSELF in just minutes. We call it The One-Minute ⇥⇤ Miracle, which is a modified version of a process that was first discovered in the early 1980's by Dr. Roger Callahan, a licensed psychotherapist. No special knowledge is required to achieve success with this technique, but having an understanding of the human energy field, the meridian system, and the mind explains WHY this tool is so powerful. The One-Minute ⇥⇤ Miracle is the very FIRST thing we teach you to master in our Level I Miracle Mastery ⇥⇤ Program, because it rapidly clears self-sabotaging blocks that are trapped in your cellular memory. Although it is very QUICK and extremely EASY to do, it is probably the most powerful healing tool I have ever seen in my entire 59 years of being on the planet. It's difficult to grasp the value of this concept until you actually EXPERIENCE it for yourself. This is why we take you by the hand and walk you through it in ways that are SIMPLE TO UNDERSTAND and EASY TO DO. I only wish I would have discovered it SOONER!

How to be Happy REGARDLESS of Circumstances

This is simple, because Life is what you CHOOSE to make it — so why not choose to make it FUN? First, APPRECIATE everything that IS working well in your life then make it your ONGOING INTENTION to find ways to see the BEAUTY and BENEFITS in ALL of Life's circumstances. The more you focus on the GOOD, the more GOODNESS you are likely to experience in your life. Consciously intend to become "The Happiest Person You Know!"

How to Become the
Most Popular Person on the Planet

If you ever read *How to Win Friends and Influence People* by Dale Carnegie, you already know the value of being a GOOD LISTENER. The two things that most people value MORE than anything else are: 1) the opportunity to talk about things they LOVE, and 2) having someone take the time to really LISTEN to what they have to say. To help bring out the HIGHEST NATURE in others, ask them this thought-provoking question:

"What do you like best about _____?"

Ask them what they like best about their JOB, their MATE, their HOBBIES, or SPECIAL INTERESTS, etc. You can also invite them to tell you about their HIGHEST ASPIRATIONS and BIGGEST DREAMS. Listening to others share things of a positive nature is one of the greatest gifts you can give to someone, because it causes their energy to go UP and their spirits to RISE. Giving someone your UNDIVIDED ATTENTION and inviting them to SHARE their joy and enthusiasm with you, automatically JUMPSTARTS their immune system (as well as your own), which is another valuable benefit of being a good listener. What we are about to share next will inspire others to regard you as "World's Greatest Conversationalist!" Watch what happens when you use these **9 Magic Words**:

"Do you know what I like about you, _____?"

People will literally be sitting on the edge of their seats as they eagerly await your response. When you SINCERELY acknowledge their POSITIVE ATTRIBUTES, you will most likely see them demonstrate even MORE of whatever you have praised them for, because they want to LIVE UP TO your high expectations of their magnificence. We invite you to experiment with these ideas, because they are likely to cause your OWN sense of well-being to MULTIPLY EXPONENTIALLY. When you make it a HABIT to use these **9 Magic Words** with everyone you meet each day, you will soon become "The Most POPULAR Person on the Planet!" When applying these principles, please remember...

Sincerity is the **key**.

Time-Tested

...that which has been
consistently proven over time
to have measurable value.

Time-Tested Tips and 米 Techniques

The recommendations below are intended to **amplify** your personal power and **accelerate** the rate at which 𝕿𝖍𝖊 15-𝓜𝖎𝖓𝖚𝖙𝖊 米 𝓜𝖎𝖗𝖆𝖈𝖑𝖊 works for **YOU**!

Start off your day in the most powerful way: Before you even open your eyes in the morning, GIVE THANKS for the things you might otherwise take for granted. The more you REALIZE how fortunate you ALREADY ARE, the more fortunate you BECOME.

Make a commitment to joy: Make it your top priority to find ways to become "The Happiest Person You Know." When you are HAPPY, your health IMPROVES, your relationships THRIVE, and your prosperity GROWS. This soon becomes "The Story of Your Life!"

Create a rewarding habit: Give yourself permission to go to a quiet place each day to INDULGE in your 15-𝓜𝖎𝖓𝖚𝖙𝖊 米 𝓜𝖎𝖗𝖆𝖈𝖑𝖊. When you take just 1% of your day (15 minutes) to acknowledge the wonders of Life, the other 99% of your day FLOWS more gracefully.

Take a 21-Day "Creation Vacation:" The easiest way to master 𝕿𝖍𝖊 15-𝓜𝖎𝖓𝖚𝖙𝖊 米 𝓜𝖎𝖗𝖆𝖈𝖑𝖊 is to indulge in it at least 5 TIMES A WEEK for a month. By then it becomes like an OLD FRIEND who is always there to inspire you and make it easier for you to find your way.

Do it first thing in the morning: This is ideal, because it PAVES the way to a wonderful day. Another good time to write is just before you go to bed at night, because whatever you think of just before you fall asleep is processed by your subconscious ALL NIGHT long.

Write it down: Studies show that those who commit their dreams and desires to PAPER greatly increase the odds of achieving their goals and attracting more income. It's amazing that such a SMALL investment of time could yield such HIGH dividends!

Listen to IT (InTuition): The INITIAL thought that you have when doing each step of your 15-𝓜𝖎𝖓𝖚𝖙𝖊 米 𝓜𝖎𝖗𝖆𝖈𝖑𝖊 is usually your **InTuition** delivering a valuable message to you. Even if you don't understand it at first, it's best to acknowledge it and write it down.

Keep your thoughts purely positive: To attract and create the life of your dreams, it is ESSENTIAL that you think in PURELY POSITIVE terms. Remember…"What you FILL your mind with your life is FULL of," so fill your mind with PURELY POSITIVE thoughts.

Learn by example: Feel totally free to COPY the examples in any of our books until you feel confident doing 𝕿𝖍𝖊 15-Minute ⭒ Miracle on your own. Many people tell us they get EXTRAORDINARY results writing them down WORD for WORD.

You always get to be RIGHT: Life supports you 100% and AGREES with EVERYTHING you say. Before you create your statements and/or declarations, be sure to pause and ask yourself this important question: "What do I want to be RIGHT about TODAY?"

You only need to write it down once: Although you may choose to write the same thing OVER and OVER AGAIN until you see evidence that your request has been heard, you really only need to write it ONCE for Life to ACKNOWLEDGE it and ACT upon it.

Do it YOUR way: Each 15-Minute ⭒ Miracle can have a SINGLE theme for the entire process or each step can have a theme of its OWN. Either way is appropriate. Do whatever feels best to YOU on any given day.

Maximize your benefits: For the best possible results, PAUSE after writing each segment of your 15-Minute ⭒ Miracle and INHALE deeply then EXHALE slowly. Double check to make SURE that the statements you are making are causing your energy to go UP.

Double your pleasure: By sharing your 15-Minute ⭒ Miracle with a PARTNER, you greatly boost your odds of success. When you WRITE IT and READ IT back, you also get to HEAR IT. When you SHARE IT with another person, you BOTH benefit exponentially.

Read it just before you go to bed: If you read your daily 15-Minute ⭒ Miracle masterpiece just before you retire at night, you are likely to ACCELERATE the rate at which it works wonders in your life. Better yet, read it ALOUD into a tape recorder and play it back.

Release attachments: Upon completing your 15-Minute ⭒ Miracle, you are likely to enjoy Life's grandest plan when you simply RELEASE and let go of any attachment to HOW and WHEN things manifest. Just LET GO and LET **GoD** take care of the DETAILS!

Stay in the flow: The quickest and easiest way to regain your BALANCE and get back into the FLOW of Life is to find something (anything) to APPRECIATE. It is literally IMPOSSIBLE to experience negative emotion while practicing the ATTITUDE of GRATITUDE.

Appreciation is the key: The expression of gratitude is the KEY that opens the door to personal fulfillment. This is the most significant step in the entire 15-Minute ⋇ Miracle process, because it sets the stage for all the OTHER steps to elevate the quality of your life.

Appreciate even the smallest of things: Life brings second helpings of everything you LOVE and APPRECIATE. Therefore take the time to express GRATITUDE for even the SMALLEST of things. Anything you can do on a SMALL scale, you can also do on a GRAND scale!

Understand the Law of Inclusion: It is impossible to EXCLUDE anything from your life. Whatever you give your attention to with FEELING is automatically INCLUDED as part of your life experience, so be very SELECTIVE about your thoughts, words, and feelings.

Life is one big shopping spree: Whatever you think about, talk about, observe, and imagine, NON-SELECTIVELY jumps into your shopping cart for you to take home — even things you may NOT WANT! Therefore, focus ONLY upon what you DO WANT!

Notice how you feel: Your Inner Guidance System communicates with you through your feelings. When you feel a sense of COMFORT, you are in the flow of Life. When you feel DISCOMFORT, Life is just inviting you to find something to APPRECIATE.

Let Life take care of the details: CLARIFY how you love to FEEL and ENVISION living "the life of your dreams." Ask to experience Life's grandest plan and invite it to unfold in just the PERFECT TIME and in DELIGHTFUL WAYS that BENEFIT All Life Everywhere.

Expect a Miracle: "As you BELIEVE, so shall it BE." There seems to be a direct correlation between what you EXPECT and what you EXPERIENCE in life. In fact, "What you EXPECT is what you GET!" This is why we make it our daily practice to EXPECT MIRACLES!

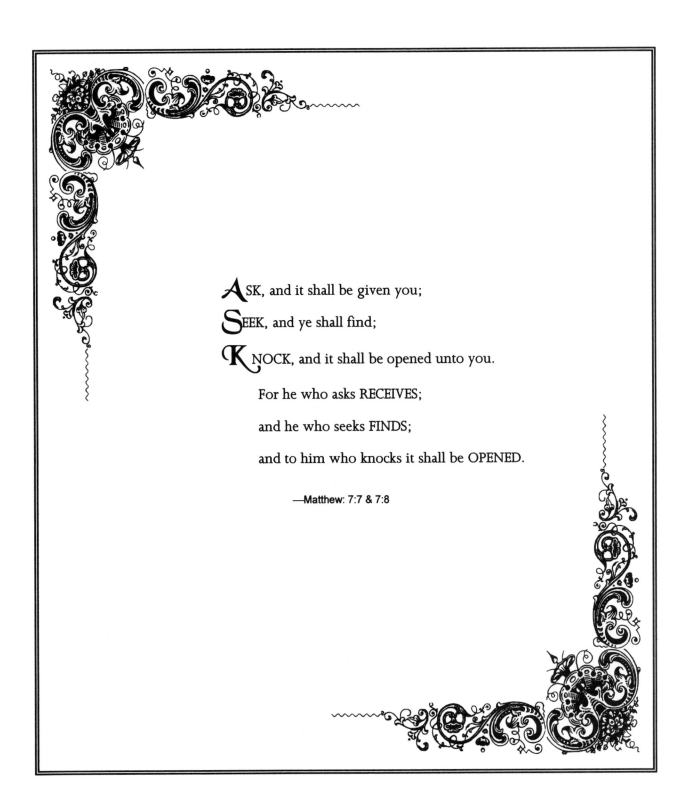

ASK, and it shall be given you;

SEEK, and ye shall find;

KNOCK, and it shall be opened unto you.

For he who asks RECEIVES;

and he who seeks FINDS;

and to him who knocks it shall be OPENED.

—Matthew: 7:7 & 7:8

If You **Don't** ✳ **Ask** You **Don't Get!**

—Mahatma Gandhi

"The fool **wonders** — the wise man **asks**."

—Benjamin Disraeli

The fascinating secrets revealed in this chapter have the potential to TRANSFORM your life in a measurably positive way VERY QUICKLY. If you are like most people, you find it difficult to ASK ANYONE for ANYTHING. Why do you suppose that is? Ron and I decided to survey a number of individuals to determine what kept them from asking for what they truly wanted in life. Below are EXAMPLES of their responses:

"I don't like criticism."

"It's too much trouble."

"Maybe I don't deserve it."

"It makes me uncomfortable."

"I would rather do it all myself."

"Someone might think I am ignorant."

"I can't stand the thought of rejection."

"I don't want to be obligated to others."

We believe that DISCOMFORT in asking stems from the FEAR of not meeting with the APPROVAL of OTHERS. Perhaps we find it too PAINFUL to take the risk of being JUDGED, REJECTED, or possibly CRITICIZED. Unfortunately, this fear TOTALLY IMMOBILIZES us and causes us to stay right where we are — even when we KNOW we really don't want to be there!

Now that we have examined several reasons why NOT to ASK,
let's look to see what could happen if we DID ASK:

"I could have fun."

"I could get a job."

"I could get a raise."

"I could get new ideas."

"I could simplify my life."

"I could learn something."

"I could save a lot of time."

"I could get what I ask for."

"I could save a lot of money."

"I could increase my income."

"I could get some good advice."

"People may be delighted to help."

"I could obtain valuable information."

"I could meet new and interesting people."

"I could benefit from the experience of others."

When we examine all the BENEFITS of asking, it appears to be something worth considering. The next logical step is to figure out WHOM and HOW to ask. To truly master the art of asking, we highly recommend you read *The Aladdin Factor* by Jack Canfield and Mark Victor Hansen (the *Chicken Soup for the Soul* geniuses). This book will definitely help you find COURAGE and COMFORT in asking for anything your heart truly desires. Since the SECRET behind 𝕿𝖍𝖊 15-Minute ✟ Miracle is learning how to ASK, it may be well worth your time to become really GOOD at it. Start by asking for simple things like ADVICE or DIRECTIONS. When you become comfortable with those two things, then begin to ask for ASSISTANCE from time to time. Before long, ASKING will be very EASY for you.

How to Land the Job of Your Dreams by Asking for Advice

This next revelation is extremely FUN and REWARDING. It definitely has the potential to SUPERCHARGE your life — in fact; this idea alone may be worth the price of this book! It is appropriately referred to as the ADVICE CALL and is one of the most extraordinary concepts I have ever come across in my entire life. Allow me to give you an example of how I used this amazing door-opening technique when I needed to find a way to make a major change in my employment.

When I was in my early 30's, I was STUCK in a hopeless rut with regard to my job. Although I didn't like being there, I had NO IDEA where I wanted to go. Because I had NO SOLUTIONS of my own, I ended up investing thousands of dollars to retain the services of a reputable executive guidance firm. This ultimately led to a most enlightening discovery.

After ascertaining which career possibilities I wanted to investigate, I researched to find out who were the TOP achievers in these areas of endeavor. I then wrote a short letter congratulating them on their impressive accomplishments and politely requested 15 minutes of their time to seek their expert ADVICE. Knowing they were very busy, I usually offered to take them out to lunch. I began by telling them how much I admired them as positive role models, and then I went on to say, "My goal is to EXCEL in the field of _____, and I am seeking EXPERT ADVICE from those who have already PROVEN to be very successful. This is why I specifically want to talk with YOU, _____."

The results were absolutely ASTOUNDING! Not only did many of them offer me valuable inside information, but some of them even offered me a JOB. If they couldn't help me personally, they often took the time to arrange additional interviews with their colleagues. Everywhere I went I received tremendous HELP and SUPPORT from people I had never even met before. My sense of SELF-WORTH just skyrocketed. As I began to consciously appreciate my OWN attributes, others responded to me with much higher regard. They made me feel as though I really had something of enormous VALUE to offer. Within two weeks, my biggest problem was no longer wondering if I would ever receive a decent job offer, but rather deciding WHICH ONE to accept! Now when I want to move forward in any area of my life and have a lot of fun doing it, I just make one advice call after the other. It's not only a lot of FUN, but it's also extremely REWARDING. You'll be absolutely AMAZED at the results!

The whole purpose of telling you this story is to emphasize the value of ASKING for ADVICE and ASSISTANCE. Most people are absolutely THRILLED when asked for their opinion on something. They consider it a COMPLIMENT that you are interested in their point of view, and they usually have a sincere desire to be of SERVICE to you.

Just for fun, you might like to make a PRACTICE ADVICE CALL so you can see for yourself how EASY it is. Pretend you are a reporter and that you are writing a story to help your readers discover the most effective way to become self-employed. Now find the most extraordinary ROLE MODEL you can — a very SUCCESSFUL ENTREPRENEUR. Next, write this person a letter explaining who you are and telling them that you have a burning desire to ALSO become self-employed. Promise to take not more than 15 MINUTES of their time to have them answer just THREE QUESTIONS that will very likely make an enormous positive difference in your life. It is advisable to call your prospects and offer to take them out for lunch if you desire more than a few minutes of their time. Make up a list of QUESTIONS that will make it EASY for your interviewees to give you the information you desire.

After COMPLETING your advice call, you have a SECOND opportunity to create a favorable impression by sending a handwritten THANK-YOU NOTE within 24 hours. Most importantly, release your ATTACHMENT to the outcome. Just have FUN with this playful process. This is one of the QUICKEST and EASIEST ways I have ever found to comfortably develop an enormous amount of COURAGE, SELF-CONFIDENCE, and ENTHUSIASM. Throw all caution to the wind and JUST DO IT! The fastest way to overcome your fear of ASKING is to completely DISREGARD the OUTCOME and make it your PRIMARY INTENTION to just GATHER DATA. If something good comes out of it, this is GREAT. It not, you still have MORE INFORMATION and EXPERIENCE than you had before! Either way, YOU WIN!

Go for it! 👍

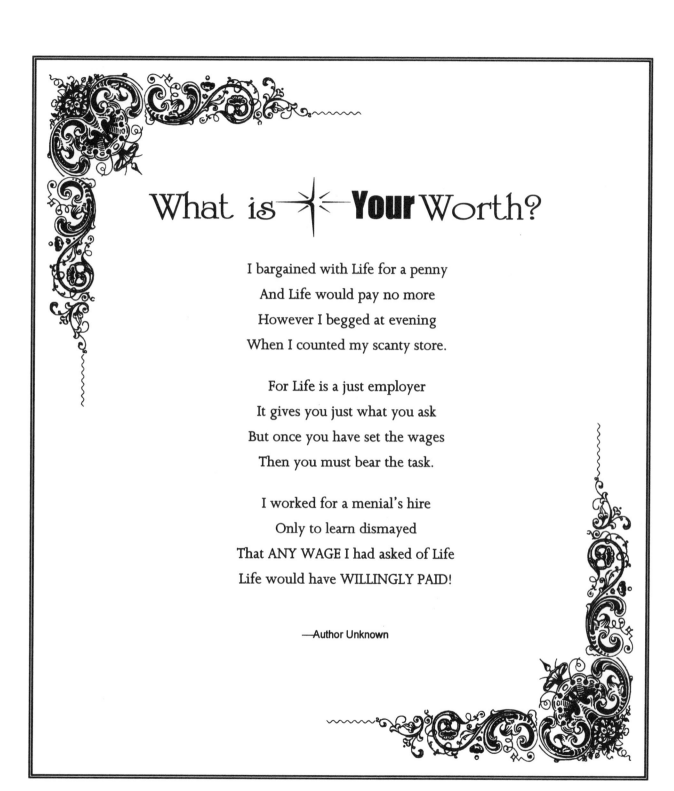

What is ✴ **Your** Worth?

I bargained with Life for a penny
And Life would pay no more
However I begged at evening
When I counted my scanty store.

For Life is a just employer
It gives you just what you ask
But once you have set the wages
Then you must bear the task.

I worked for a menial's hire
Only to learn dismayed
That ANY WAGE I had asked of Life
Life would have WILLINGLY PAID!

—Author Unknown

✴ Unconditional Love

...**total acceptance**, not
limited in any way by conditions
or qualifications. Our Creator loves
each one of us unconditionally.

The Liberating ✳ Law of Allowing

"Live and let live."

Wouldn't it be marvelous if other people would ACCEPT us just the way we ARE? Wouldn't it be wonderful to know that we are LOVED and NOT JUDGED in any way as we joyfully CHOOSE our life experiences? Although we may not always meet with everyone's APPROVAL 100% of the time, there IS a way to encourage people to demonstrate their highest nature MOST of the time. **Here's the secret:** Whenever you observe another person, REGARDLESS of who it is, make a point to SAY TO YOURSELF as you go through your day:

> "I AM that which I AM, and I am WILLING to
> **allow** all others to BE that which they ARE."
>
> —Jerry and Esther Hicks

This INSTANTLY relieves you of the need to JUDGE or CONTROL the actions of others. This is, without a doubt, the BIGGEST KEY to giving and receiving UNCONDITIONAL LOVE. This non-judgmental expression of acceptance is best demonstrated by our animal friends. That's why I aspire to become "the AWESOME PERSON my dog THINKS I am!" Let's take YOUR pet for example: Have you ever noticed how he or she totally ADORES you no matter WHAT you do, HOW you look, or HOW you act? The reason most people are so devoted to their animals is because their loyal companions NEVER judge them. Animals are extraordinary role models for us to emulate, because they INSTINCTIVELY love their human friends NO MATTER WHAT! This is what we call UNCONDITIONAL LOVE in its purest form —loving another both BECAUSE OF and IN SPITE OF prevailing conditions!

When you begin to express these warm and wonderful feelings toward the REST of your human family, you will find that they, just like your loving animal buddies, will be much more inclined to ACCEPT YOU just the way you are. **The bottom line is this:** When you release YOUR need to judge and control OTHERS, then others will be more inclined to release THEIR need to judge and control YOU. When you employ this simple philosophy, you may discover that it feels much better to be IN LOVE than to be IN CONTROL!

The truest test of loving unconditionally is to love others even when they display LESS than unconditional love toward YOU. Even if others PERSIST in judging YOU, just continue to ALLOW them to think and believe as they CHOOSE. They are undoubtedly doing the very BEST they can with their current level of understanding of how Life works. Please know that if they COULD do better, they certainly WOULD do better. And if **YOU** could do better, **YOU** would certainly do better TOO!

Even bestowing GIFTS upon loved ones calls for an expression of UNCONDITIONAL LOVE. When you lovingly GIVE something to someone (with NO STRINGS attached), we call this "GIVING A GIFT." When, however, you INSIST on someone having something they really don't even want, we call this "IMPOSING YOUR AGENDA upon someone else!" So if you truly want to retain your INTEGRITY when giving someone a gift…

Be sure to give them something **they** want,
and not something **you** want for them!

Even though unconditional love may not be so easy to practice AT FIRST, the benefits are well worth your effort to become GOOD at it. When others love YOU unconditionally, they naturally bring out the BEST in you, which inspires YOU to love OTHERS in the same way. When you make a practice of ACCEPTING others, (REGARDLESS of what they say or do), they tend to respond to you in a much KINDER manner. Perhaps this sounds like "following the path of LEAST resistance." We, however, advocate "following the path of NO resistance!"

Each of us moves through our life experience in our OWN TIME and in our OWN WAY. As long as you HONOR the sacred space of others, you will likely experience a sense of well-being that allows YOU to be happy, REGARDLESS of what other people say or do. Unless others are violating YOUR sacred space, it's best to ALLOW them to express their uniqueness as they explore Life at their OWN PACE. It is also important to realize that this is not the same as merely "tolerating" them. When you are truly ALLOWING, you feel a comforting sense of HARMONY and CONTENTMENT. When, however, you merely TOLERATE someone's behavior, you will surely feel NEGATIVE EMOTION, which inadvertently blocks your OWN flow of pure positive energy. It's easy to know whether you are ALLOWING or just TOLERATING. All you have to do is just NOTICE how you FE-E-E-E-EL.

Let's take a moment to figure out ways to FREE ourselves from negative emotions that UNDERMINE our joy. Until we FORGIVE OURSELVES for unwise choices we made in the past, we allow GUILT to rob us of our joy. Likewise, until we find it in our hearts to FORGIVE OTHERS for unwise choices they may have made in the past, we allow RESENTMENT, JEALOUSY, and BLAME to actually keep us from realizing our goals. These TOXIC EMOTIONS also seriously jeopardize our HEALTH. We can RELIEVE ourselves of these stressful feelings by simply RELEASING our negative judgment and ALLOWING Life to carry out whatever justice is appropriate. You'll most likely feel 1,000 pounds LIGHTER as you engage in the empowering process below:

"I am now willing to release and let go of the anger and resentment I have toward _____, and I agree to allow whoever CAUSED these negative emotions to experience whatever consequences BELONG to him or her. May all negativity be returned to the Universe harmless and formless and TRANSFORMED into the pure positive energy of LOVE."

This implies that JUSTICE is somehow being served, which allows most people to feel better RIGHT AWAY. As you embrace the principles of *The 15-Minute* ⭐ *Miracle*, however, you will probably graduate to the method outlined in the NEXT example. In the meantime, please feel free to use the previous technique as a BRIDGE until you no longer feel the need for it.

"I am ready to release and let go of my need to BLAME OTHERS for any undesirable conditions in my life. I now choose to take FULL RESPONSIBILITY for creating my OWN sense of worth and well-being, because I finally realize that **I** have the power to attract and create the life I PREFER. From now on, I choose to invite a warm sense of HARMONY and BALANCE into my life. Starting today, I choose to CELEBRATE my blessings and find JOY and DELIGHT in every moment as it magically unfolds."

Until we release and let go of the PAST, we will never be truly FREE to
enjoy the present moment — and the PRESENT is all we really have. Remember…

There is **no future** in the **past**!

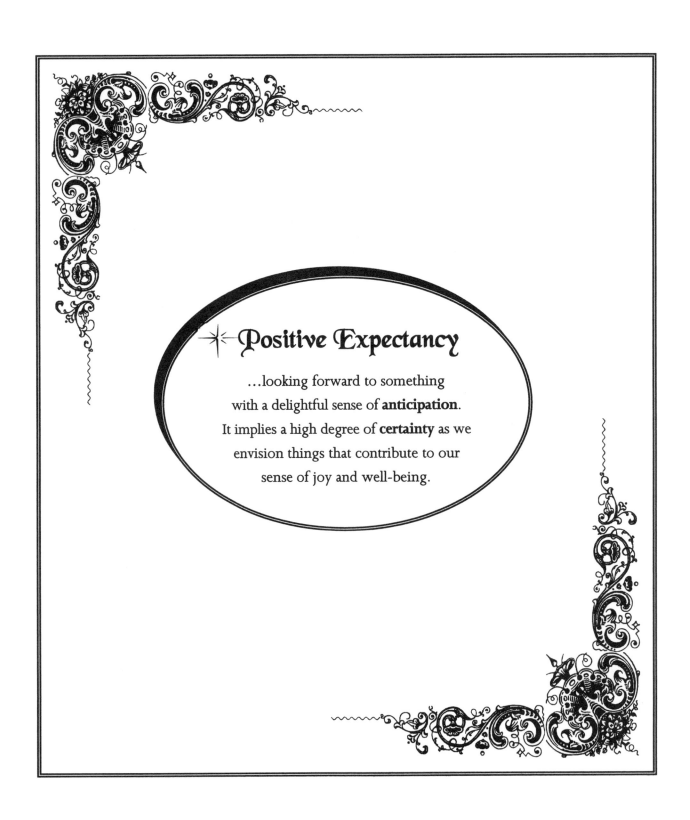

Positive Expectancy

…looking forward to something
with a delightful sense of **anticipation**.
It implies a high degree of **certainty** as we
envision things that contribute to our
sense of joy and well-being.

The Powerful Law
of ⚹ Positive Expectancy

"Expect a ⚹ Miracle"

—Dan Wakefield

Since recorded history, healers and physicians have successfully utilized PLACEBOS to heal the body because they have proven to produce AMAZING RESULTS. Placebos are simply neutral preparations (like sugar pills) that are given in order to comfort patients who feel ill or deficient in some way. It is interesting to note that the literal Latin translation of the word "placebo" is "I SHALL PLEASE." When the mind really BELIEVES that a pill or procedure will provide a CURE, the body immediately RESPONDS by producing the necessary chemicals, hormones, and drugs to HEAL itself. When you begin to grasp the significance of this idea, you are better able to deliberately create more FAVORABLE circumstances in your life. For a more thorough understanding of the power of believing, we highly recommend that you read *Your Body Believes Every Word You Say* by Barbara H. Levine, *The Magic of Believing* by Claude M. Bristol, and a little book entitled *As a Man Thinketh* by James Allen.

There is a humorous example of this phenomenon demonstrated by a woman who had such great difficulty sleeping that she had to obtain a prescription for SLEEPING PILLS. Her doctor assured her, if she would take a couple of these pills just prior to retiring for the evening, that she would enjoy a RESTFUL SLEEP and wake up refreshed. That night she took TWO PILLS and literally slept like a baby. She was puzzled, however, when she awoke to find the SAME TWO PILLS still lying on the nightstand next to her bed. Then she suddenly remembered that she had promised to sew TWO BUTTONS on her husband's shirt and noticed that both buttons were MISSING (talk about the "Potent Power of Placebos" and the "Powerful Law of Positive Expectancy")!

"But how can I **believe** in that which I've not yet **seen**?"

149

The answer lies in simply TRUSTING that the laws of the Universe DO work and that they WILL work for YOU. As Dr. Wayne Dyer says, "You'll SEE it when you BELIEVE it!" If you BELIEVE in the Law of Gravity and the Law of Magnetic Attraction, you can be 100% SURE that The 15-Minute ☀ Miracle can and WILL work for YOU!

Most of us cannot explain HOW electricity works, yet we USE it nearly every day of our lives. We EXPECT that when we plug in a lamp and turn it on, that we shall have light. The 15-Minute ☀ Miracle operates on that same principle. Even if you do not understand the nuts-and-bolts of HOW it works, you can still plug into it and BENEFIT from it as often as you like. The best part is that this magical process has been divinely designed to consistently work in YOUR favor — all you have to do is follow the easy-to-apply principles and just be WILLING TO ACCEPT the goodness that Life wants you to have.

It doesn't seem to matter whether you UNDERSTAND The 15-Minute ☀ Miracle or even BELIEVE in it — it seems to work ANYWAY! It works BEST, however, when you do the process as outlined in this book, then completely RELEASE YOUR ATTACHMENT to the outcome. This is definitely a MAJOR KEY to manifesting miracles in your life. I personally experience the most favorable results when I just have FUN and PLAY with this process. When I deeply LONG for something, I unavoidably attract more LACK and LIMITATION into my life. This is because I am so focused upon what I DON'T HAVE. When I simply APPRECIATE today's blessings and BASK in the positive possibilities of tomorrow, I consistently experience results that amaze and delight me. The best news is that YOU can do the same thing! If you want to gain even FURTHER benefit, share some of these inspiring ideas with others. The more you explain it to OTHER people, the better you will understand it YOURSELF. Before long, you will be a highly sought-after **B.o.L.**

"**Bringer of Light.**"

150

You **Can** If You **THINK** You **Can**!

If you THINK you are beaten, you are
If you THINK you dare not, you don't
If you like to win, but you THINK you can't
It's almost certain you won't.

If you THINK you'll lose, you've lost
For out in the world we find
Success begins with a person's will
It's all in the state of mind.

If you THINK you are outclassed, you are
You've got to THINK high to rise
You've got to be sure of yourself before
You ever can win the prize.

Life's triumphs don't always go
To the stronger or faster man
But sooner or later the man who wins
Is the man who THINKS he can!

Quoted from *The Spice of Life* by Dian Ritter

If you don't
have love for **yourself**,
you can't be loving
to **others**.

—Dr. Wayne Dyer

If I Only Knew Then What I Know → ⸭← Now

Recently, while doing some spring-cleaning and organizing my files, I happened to find something I never even realized I had. I was so thrilled to discover this unexpected gift, as it offered me a sweet bouquet of FRESH POSSIBILITIES to consider. "What was this intriguing and delightful treasure?" you ask. It was a warm and inviting LETTER of WELCOME from "The Loving Power that Created All That Is" entitled...

Instructions for Living a Happy Life

Because it took me quite a while to figure things out, I had to learn the lessons of Life the HARD way. I probably could have saved a lot of time and trouble if only I had read these instructions much earlier. Until I embraced these loving words of wisdom, I was thoroughly convinced it was socially inappropriate to focus upon my OWN needs and desires. I was taught, from a very early age, that this was WRONG and was considered to be SELFISH. What I neglected to realize was that I couldn't possibly GIVE anything to others that I did not HAVE myself. I could never become SICK enough to make another person WELL, POOR enough to make someone else RICH, nor DUMB enough to make anyone SMART. I now know that "The MORE I have, the MORE I have to give" and that "The more I have to GIVE, the more I love to LIVE!"

While we are certainly not suggesting that you ever be selfish, we want to emphasize how BENEFICIAL it is for you to be LOVING and ACCEPTING of YOURSELF. It is absolutely ESSENTIAL to allow Life to fill YOUR cup to overflowing so you are in a better position to help others fill THEIRS. By acknowledging my OWN strengths, I was able to be of much greater value to everyone else. I finally figured out that it's IMPOSSIBLE to pour from an EMPTY CUP! Now that MY cup runneth over, I just love encouraging others to allow Life to fill THEIR cups with abundant LOVE, LIGHT, and PROSPERITY. Once THEY become inspired, they are most eager to enlighten and support OTHERS. By the way, would you like to see the original **Instructions for Living a Happy Life** (as if you had a choice)?

Instructions

for Living a ✦ Happy Life

Welcome, Magnificent One!

We have been eagerly awaiting your arrival, as everyone here acknowledges how very special you are. You could not have come at a more opportune time! The world is going through many dramatic and exciting changes and looks forward to your unique participation in this wonderful ✦ Game of Life. You are hereby invited to claim your **personal birthrights** *that are meant for you to enjoy for an entire lifetime:*

You were born:

to be absolutely **magnificent**,

to be as **happy** *as you are willing to be*

with **freedom of choice** *to use as you see fit,*

to enjoy **perfect health** *of body, mind, and spirit,*

to enjoy great **abundance** *of all things that are good,*

to be a **shining light** *of happiness for others to emulate,*

to learn only the **Truth** *and offer it to others who are seeking;*

to enjoy perfect **balance** *as you play and discover the wonders of life,*

to partake in whatever uplifts your spirits, then to **share** *it with others,*

to **l♥ve yourself** *unconditionally and, in turn,* **l♥ve** *others in the same way.*

In short, you were born to shine your light in the world and **enjoy** *abundant*

✦ *Health* ✦ *Happiness* ✦ *Harmony* ✦ *Peace* ✦ *Playfulness*

✦ *Prosperity* ✦ *L♥ve* ✦ *Beauty* ✦ *Joy.*

Your primary mission in Life is to discover what really delights you and to focus ALL of your attention upon that. This enables Life to l♥vingly offer you a perfect sense of balance, comfort, and well-being. Disregard those who do not understand Life and accuse you of being selfish. Others may not yet know that you can only be of benefit to them (and to all others) when you have learned to l♥ve and appreciate YOURSELF. When you are happy:

- ♥ *Your relationships tend to blossom and grow with ease.*
- ♥ *You want everyone else to discover their own happiness.*
- ♥ *You find you are eager to share your abundance with everyone.*
- ♥ *Your health approaches perfection, so you are a greater asset to all.*
- ♥ *Your energy level increases, so you can be of greater service to others.*

The most altruistic thing you can do is to engage in that which truly makes your heart sing — then acknowledge all of your blessings and bask in the positive possibilities that abound. When you do this, My Loving Angel, you will be of extraordinary value to All Life Everywhere. You will naturally want to share and circulate your abundance.

*There is only ✳←**L♥ve** for you here in the Universe. It is up to you to either accept it or reject it...however, ✳←**L♥ve** is all there is. Please know that you actually can be, do, and have absolutely anything your heart desires. Just CLAIM your gift of abundance, BASK in the positive anticipation of receiving it, and KNOW that it's on its way. When you go forth and seek joy, everything else falls into place perfectly. You, My Exquisite Masterpiece, are my Perfect Creation in whom I am well pleased! You are a ✳← Divine Expression of Pure Perfection.*

*With Unconditional ✳←**L♥ve** and ✳← Unlimited Support,*

✳← The L♥ving Power that Created All That Is

⊔

If you truly want to **realize** it,
all you have to do is 𝓜𝓲𝓻𝓪𝓬𝓵𝓮-𝓲𝔃𝓮 it!

—Heathcliff Aldana —⊁← S.o.L.

Part 7

- ♥ Can You Come Out and Play?
- ♥ Miracle →‖← Mastery Program (Levels I-III)
- ♥ The Positive Power of 3 Program (Private Playshop)
- ♥ Miracle Discovery Groups with Volunteer Facilitators
- ♥ The Deluxe Miracle Starter Kit
- ♥ 100% Satisfaction →‖← Guarantee
- ♥ Bibliography — Inspirational Food for Thought

Can You Come Out and ✳ Play?

At least four times a year, we offer a variety of Playshops at our ranch in Los Gatos, California, where the country air smells exceptionally fresh and clean. The mountain views are absolutely beautiful and the energy surrounding the Summit Sunrise Ranch seems almost magical among the majestic oaks and redwoods that are indigenous to this area. The Pacific Ocean is only 15 miles away and it takes just 90 minutes to drive to San Francisco.

People come from near and far to renew their spirits and discover an amazingly simple way to **fall in love** — in love with Life and everything in it, INCLUDING THEMSELVES! Many literally ignite with delight when they begin to realize all of the wonderful possibilities that are available to them. When you make the conscious connection between "what you THINK" and "what you EXPERIENCE," you can consciously CHOOSE the quality of your life. Once you discover how you UNINTENTIONALLY attract UNWANTED circumstances into your life, you can then more DELIBERATELY attract that which you PREFER instead. This new-found awareness enables you to take your rightful place in the DRIVER'S SEAT of LIFE! If you prefer "foresight" over "hindsight," you'll be very glad you came.

If you are inspired to participate in any of our activities, please feel free to call us at (408) 353-2050 to make the necessary arrangements. Because our gatherings are very experiential, we like to keep our groups relatively small. For that reason, you may want to reserve your space well in advance. If you require overnight accommodations, please visit www.LosGatos.com and search for "Hotels." Life offers each of us UNLIMITED POTENTIAL, and there are MULTITUDES of MIRACLES just waiting for YOU to call them forth.

The Miracle ✳ Mastery Program™

Level I – This informative and entertaining 2-day Playshop is designed to make it easy for you to MASTER three empowering life-enhancement tools that inspire you to become "The Happiest Person You Know!" First you will learn **The One-Minute ✳ Miracle**™, which quickly FREES you from the toxic effects of fear, anxiety, resentment, disappointment, self-sabotage and more. Next you will learn the **Universal Language of Life**, which teaches you to clearly communicate your desires in ways that promise to surprise and delight you. The highlight of this unique program is discovering how to attract and create remarkable MIRACLES on a consistent basis by mastering a simple "fill-in-the-blanks journaling process" called **The 15-Minute ✳ Miracle**™. Most people are utterly amazed at the positive shift that takes place for them — often at the speed of thought!

Level II – This 2-day Miracle ✳ Mastery Playshop picks up where Level I leaves off. Here you will receive ADDITIONAL tools for transformation. Our primary focus will be on COMPLETELY MASTERING three very simple yet powerful processes called **Setups for Success, Compatibility Magic,** and **The Million-Dollar Mindset.** Learning to skillfully utilize these practical life management tools empowers you to SET UP your life to MATCH your DESIRES with amazing ease and grace. After this weekend, you'll have all the tools you need to become an "Irresistible Magnet for Miracles."

Level III – **The Elite Retreat**™ is a fabulous "Creation Vacation" aboard a beautiful luxury cruise ship that caters to your utmost comfort and well-being. For 2-3 days you will have the opportunity to CLEANSE your body, CLEAR your mind, and CLAIM your spirit by completely rewriting **The Story of Your Life.** For the other 4-5 days of your journey, you will be free to partake of other activities on the ship and visit the various ports of call. Because **The Elite Retreat**™ is Level III of the Miracle ✳ Mastery Program, you must have completed at least LEVEL I before you are properly prepared to participate in this event. Level II is also RECOMMENDED, but NOT REQUIRED.

Please see the following pages for more complete
information on The Miracle ✳ Mastery Program™.

Level I Playshop
Miracle  Mastery Program™
Clear the Deck…Clarify Your Desires…and Create the Life You Love

"Why is it that some people are RICH, HAPPY, and HEALTHY, while others are POOR, DEPRESSED, and ILL? What does the top 3% of our nation's population know that the other 97% doesn't? How can the AVERAGE PERSON find that elusive sense of personal fulfillment that we all long to experience?" If you would like to know the answers to these and other compelling questions, you stand to benefit greatly from attending the **Level I Miracle  Mastery Playshop™**. In a single weekend you will learn how to…

- Access comfort and peace of mind at the speed of thought!

- Turn stumbling blocks into valuable steppingstones very quickly!

- Tap into and use the innate wisdom and genius that resides within you!

- Replace your negative programming with "A Whole New Story of Your Life!"

- Reap enormous benefits by learning to master the "Universal Language of Life!"

- Use "9 Magic Words" that will make you the most popular person on the planet!

- Master 7 simple steps that make it easy for you to achieve your goals more quickly!

Many of our clients have told us that this empowering course has done more to help them regain their comfort, confidence, and vitality for Life than anything they have ever experienced. They are amazed that something so SIMPLE and FUN could have such PROFOUND effects in ALL areas of their lives. After one weekend, you will finally have the tools you need to access the ANSWERS, SOLUTIONS, and GENIUS residing within you that are eager to emerge. The Level I Miracle  Mastery Playshop is a 2-day event that you are likely to remember for the rest of your life. Your satisfaction is **100% guaranteed!**

Level II Playshop
Miracle ✷ Mastery Program™

How to **Set Up Your Life** to **Match Your Desires**

Do TIME, MONEY, and SUCCESS seem to elude you no matter how FAST you run, how LONG you work, or how HARD you try? Are you sick and tired of feeling overwhelmed while working so HARD to accomplish so LITTLE? Do you ever wish you had more TIME and ENERGY available to do what you REALLY want to do? If so, you would benefit greatly from attending the **Level II Miracle** ✷ **Mastery Playshop™**. In only two days you will learn how to...

- Miracle-ize all of your relationships with "Compatibility Magic!"

- Release and let go of all false beliefs that keep money just beyond your reach!

- Create a relationship with yourself that will cause others to sit up and take notice!

- Find practical ways to DO what you LOVE and LOVE what you DO for a living!

- Miraculously attract more unexpected income and delightful surprises than ever before!

- Create a "Life Plan" that invites your goals to be realized and your dreams to come true!

- Master a simple yet powerful tool for transformation called "Setups for Success!"

This life-altering course will show you how to have fun creating your "Ideal Life Plan" while helping you to develop a "Million-Dollar Mindset." These tools will make it much easier for you to attract both spiritual and material WEALTH. This event will very likely take you beyond where you have ever been before in terms of conscious awareness and deliberate creation. The Level II Miracle ✷ Mastery Playshop is a 2-day seminar that shows you how to "look for JOY in all the RIGHT places." It promises to take you from the LAUNCHING PAD to LIFTOFF in ways that defy logical explanation. Again, your satisfaction is **100% guaranteed!**

161

Level III Playshop
Miracle ✴ Mastery Program™

A Chance to Completely Rewrite "The Story of Your Life"

If you are ready to CLEANSE your body, CLEAR your mind, and CLAIM your spirit, you will benefit greatly from attending the annual **7-Day** ✴ **Elite Retreat**™ aboard a beautiful luxury cruise ship. This refreshing "Creation Vacation" is ideal if you would like to create a brand new and wonderful life for yourself. It truly promises to leave you feeling refreshed, renewed, and rejuvenated!

1) **Cleanse Your Body:** You will be lovingly pampered and served a variety of delicious-tasting, life-giving foods, which will allow your body to rest and renew itself. Everything is served with an abundance of love and appreciation. It's a wonderful way to say "thanks" to your body for taking such good care of you.

2) **Clear Your Mind:** You will have the perfect opportunity to wipe your slate clean as you release and let go of things in your life (both known and unknown) that no longer serve you in a positive way. This delightfully unique process creates infinite space for new and better things to fill your mind. Ah-h-h…a fresh new beginning…a clean slate…another chance to sing the song you came here to sing!

3) **Claim Your Spirit:** Now you can easily top off your life with abundant love, joy, and laughter as you completely rewrite **The Story of Your Life**. This is your chance to reunite with who you really are. So give yourself permission to dream the "I'm Possible Dream" and take quantum leaps toward demonstrating your magnificent potential. Create the "brand new you," and have fun becoming your own best friend!

The ✳ Positive Power of 3 Program™

A **Private** Miracle ✳ Mastery Program
for Those Who Prefer to Work **One-on-One**

This program is for the individual who wants to ACCELERATE the rate at which he or she moves forward in life. Jacquelyn Aldana and her carefully chosen staff of trained professionals are available to work with you ONE-ON-ONE by phone or in person. This uniquely personalized course consists of **3** three-hour sessions, **3** sixty-minute check-in calls between sessions, and ALL the books and materials you will need to master **3** miraculous power tools. The results that our clients are reporting have far exceeded even our OWN expectations! Below are comments that reflect their satisfaction:

> "There isn't enough money in the world to pay you for what you did for me! In the very first hour, I went from a state of "gripping fear and panic" to "total peace and confidence." I have never felt happier or more vital in my entire life!" —J.C. of San Jose, California

> "Before I began The Positive Power of 3 Program, I had totally given up on myself, on Life, and on God. In less than two weeks, my spirit has been totally renewed and I now KNOW, beyond a shadow of a doubt, that I can create the life of my dreams!" —B.C. of Fayetteville, Arkansas

> "Within the first three hours of this program, I was able to release all of the negative emotion I had carried around for over 30 years with regard to my father's death. For the first time in my life, I experienced feelings of joy and positive anticipation!" —E.R. of Sunnyvale, California

Your satisfaction is 100% guaranteed!

Our intention is to provide you with time-tested tools for transformation that are designed to help you regain your balance very QUICKLY. If you agree to apply these tools as prescribed, and you do not experience a measurable degree of positive benefits, we will cheerfully return whatever you invested (minus the cost of materials). We want you to know that there is never any risk when you invest in any of our programs or materials. OUR SUCCESS is totally dependent upon YOUR SUCCESS. That's why we are highly motivated to go MANY extra miles to make sure that you receive the BEST we have to offer!

The Miracle ✳ Discovery Program™

The 15-Minute ✳ Miracle™ 8-Week Study Group

This extremely AFFORDABLE program is conducted by carefully selected VOLUNTEER FACILITATORS who are esteemed graduates of The Miracle ✳ Mastery Program (successful completion of Level I is a minimum requirement). They have been chosen because they have a burning desire to share The 15-Minute ✳ Miracle message in ways that are both FUN and REWARDING. Because they practice what they PREACH, they are living examples of what they TEACH! The unique 8-week Miracle Discovery Course is designed to empower you to create a "living masterpiece" for yourself with the support of other positive like-minded people. By mastering the simple principles of The 15-Minute ✳ Miracle, you can expect to discover your "highest purpose for being," which enables you to achieve your goals more easily. Those who complete all eight weeks typically enjoy a far deeper sense of WELL-BEING, the byproduct of which usually results in...

- ♥ Better Health
- ♥ Greater Prosperity
- ♥ More Loving Relationships

Graduates are awarded a beautiful **Miracle Explorer Certificate** suitable for framing at the completion of the course and are then eligible to join our **Miracle Mastery ✳ Leadership Program**. This entitles them to conduct 8-Week Miracle Discovery Courses of their own once they have attended the Level I Miracle ✳ Mastery Playshop and their application has been approved. For further information about joining or facilitating a Miracle Discovery Group in YOUR area, please see our website at www.15MinuteMiracle.com.

The ✳ Deluxe Miracle Starter Kit™

Everything You Need to Master 𝕿𝖍𝖊 15-Minute ✳ Miracle at Home

For the cost of a high-quality food supplement that will nourish you for only a MONTH OR TWO, you can invest in something that will nourish you for the REST OF YOUR LIFE! This is definitely one of the best BARGAINS we have to offer (nearly 50% off the retail value). It includes three of our BEST SELLING BOOKS, a delightful SURPRISE GIFT, plus a $30 GIFT CERTIFICATE. Here is what you'll receive:

1. **The 15-Minute ✳ Miracle ™ Revealed** (*an easy-to-read "Roadmap to Personal Fulfillment" book*)
2. **The Miracle Manifestation Manual** (*a "2-Month Journal with Training Wheels and Fun Activities"*)
3. **Shortcuts to Miracles** (*a condensed, easy-to-understand "Wisdom Resource Guide"*)
4. **A Delightful Surprise Gift** (*beautiful to look at and fun to use*)
5. **A $30 Gift Certificate** (*toward other products and services*)

Having the Deluxe Miracle Starter Kit™ is the next best thing to attending one of our life-enhancing **Miracle ✳ Mastery Playshops** or enrolling in one of our **8-Week Miracle Discovery Courses**. This ALL-INCLUSIVE package contains everything you need to practice and master the simple principles of 𝕿𝖍𝖊 15-Minute ✳ Miracle. Not only is it FUN and EASY to do, but it also inspires you to feel good RIGHT AWAY. When you feel good, Life seems EASIER and more JOYFUL. When you are JOYFUL, your energy goes UP. When your energy goes UP, you naturally become an "Irresistible Magnet for Miracles!"

Satisfaction ✳ Guarantee

If for any reason I should not experience a measurable sense of well-being after faithfully doing my **15-Minute ✳ Miracle** in writing for at least 21 out of 30 days, then ♥ **Inner Wisdom Publications** agrees that I am entitled to a full refund (less shipping and handling charges) by simply returning all materials both used and unused. In other words, I am either GUARANTEED a HAPPIER, more FULFILLING life, or a REFUND of my investment!

Either way, I win!

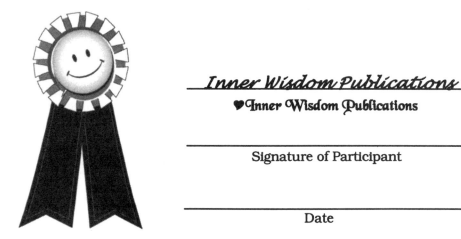

Inner Wisdom Publications

♥ Inner Wisdom Publications

_____

Signature of Participant

_____

Date

This Satisfaction Guarantee applies only for products and events offered DIRECTLY by ♥ **Inner Wisdom Publications.**

Bibliography
Inspirational Food for Thought

Aldana, Jacquelyn	The 15-Minute Miracle™ Revealed	Inner Wisdom Publications
Aldana, Jacquelyn	Miracle Manifestation Manual	Inner Wisdom Publications
Aldana, Jacquelyn	Shortcuts to Miracles	Inner Wisdom Publications
Allen, James	As a Man Thinketh	DeVorss & Company
Bach, Marcus	The World of Serendipity	Prentice-Hall
Bach, Richard	Jonathan Livingston Seagull	Avon
Blanchard, Ken	*The One-Minute Manager	Burke
Bloodworth, Venice	Key to Yourself	DeVorss Publications
Boone, J. Allen	Kinship with All Life	Harper & Row
Bristol, Claude M.	*The Magic of Believing	Cornerstone Library
Burns, David D. (M.D.)	Feeling Good — The New Mood Therapy	A Signet Book
Buscaglia, Leo	*Living, Loving, and Learning	Ballantine Books
Butterworth, Eric	Discover the Power Within You	Harper-San Francisco
Canfield and Hansen	The Aladdin Factor	Berkeley Books
Canfield and Hansen	*Chicken Soup for the Soul	Health Communications, Inc.
Carnegie, Dale	How to Win Friends and Influence People	Simon and Schuster
Chopra, Deepak (M.D.)	*Quantum Healing	Bantum
Clark, Glenn	The Man Who Tapped the Secrets of the Universe	The University of Science and Philosophy, 2000
Clark, Glenn	The Man Who Talks with the Flowers	Macalester Park Publishing Co.
Cohen, Alan	*The Dragon Doesn't Live Here Anymore	Alan Cohen Publications
Coit, Lee	*Listening	Las Brisas Retreat
Cousins, Norman	Anatomy of an Illness	Bantam
Covey, Steven R.	*7 Habits of Highly Effective People	Simon and Schuster
Dossey, Larry (M.D.)	Be Careful What You Pray For, You Just Might Get It	Harper-Collins San Francisco
Dyer, Wayne W.	*Real Magic	Harper
Dyer, Wayne W.	*You'll See It When You Believe It	Harper
Emerson, Ralph Waldo	Emerson's Essays	Thomas Crowell Company
Fisher & Robbins	Tranquility Without Pills	Bantam
Foster, Jean K.	The God-Mind Connection	Walsworth Publishing
Foundation for Inner Peace	*A Course in Miracles	Foundation for Inner Peace
Goulston and Goldberg	Get Out of Your Own Way	Perigee Books
Green, Glenda	*Love Without End	Heartwings Publishing

Hay, Louise L.	*You Can Heal Your Life	Hay House Incorporated
Hicks, Jerry and Esther	A New Beginning II	Crown International
Hill, Napoleon	*Think and Grow Rich	Ballantine Books
Jones, Debra	What You Want, Wants You	Health Comm., Inc.
Kabat-Zinn, Jon	*Wherever You Go, There You Are	Hyperion
Kipfer, Barbara Ann	14,000 Things to Be Happy About	Workman Publications
Laskow, Leonard	Healing With Love	Harper-San Fransisco
Levine, Barbara H.	Your Body Believes Every Word You Say	Aslan Publications
Lewis, Allan P.	Clearing Your Life Path	Homana Publishing
Maltz, Maxwell (M.D.)	Psycho-Cybernetics	Pocket Books of New York
Mandino, Og	*The Greatest Secret In The World	Frederick Fell, Inc.
McWilliams, Peter	*You Can't Afford the Luxury of a Negative Thought	Prelude Press
Morgan, Marlo	*Mutant Message Down Under	Harper-Collins
Mountrose, Phillip and Jane	*Getting Thru with EFT	Holistic Communications
Patent, Morgan	*You Can Have It All	Beyond Words Publishing
Peale, Norman Vincent	*The Power of Positive Thinking	Fawcett-Crest
Peale, Norman Vincent	*You Can If You Think You Can	Spire Books
Pearsall, Paul (Ph.D)	*Making Miracles	Prentice Hall Press
Ponder, Catherine	*Dare to Prosper!	Devorss & Company
Redfield, James	*The Celestine Prophecy	Warner Books, Inc.
RHJ (anonymous author)	It Works!	DeVorss & Company
Schwartz, David J.	The Magic of Thinking Big	Wilshire Book Company
Shinn, Florence Scovel	The Game of Life and How to Play It	DeVorss & Company
Siegel, Bernie (M.D.)	*Love, Medicine, & Miracles	Harper & Row
Silva and Stone	*You The Healer	Instant Improvement
Skutch, Robert	Journey Without Distance	Celestial Arts
Virtue, Doreen (Ph.D.)	I'd Change My Life If I Had the Time	Hay House Incorporated
Wakefield, Dan	Expect a Miracle	Harper-San Francisco
Walsch, Neale Donald	*Conversations with God—Books 1-3	Hampton Roads
Williamson, Marianne	*Return to Love	Harper-Collins
Winfrey (Oprah) and Green	*Make the Connection	Hyperion

*To the best of our knowledge these titles are also available on audiocassettes.
You may obtain them from your local bookseller or contact their publishers directly.

Positive Programming on Radio and Television

For 24-hour-a-day **positive programming** on TV, we recommend that you find out more about **WISDOM Television and Radio**. For further information, call 1-800-700-2212 or check out their website at www.WisdomMedia.com.

Index

About the Author

Jacquelyn Aldana lives on a small horse ranch in the Santa Cruz Mountains of sunny California (*70 miles south of San Francisco*) with her adoring husband Ron, three horses, and their beloved dog, Country Girl. She and Ron raised three exceptional sons who are each currently making a significant and positive difference in the world.

In her early years, she had numerous challenges such as chronic asthma, limited vision, moderate dyslexia, as well as symptoms of ADD. Because her parents left her at age four to be raised by her grandparents, she use to question her own sense of worthiness from time to time.

As an adult, Jacquelyn experienced many devastating circumstances that would have caused most people to jump off tall bridges, but she insists that all the contrast in her life was actually a huge BLESSING. She is deeply grateful for ALL aspects of her life, because she now is blessed to "LIVE the life she LOVES and LOVE the life she LIVES" — not IN SPITE of her challenges — but definitely BECAUSE of them! She genuinely thinks of herself as "The happiest person she knows!"

Jacquelyn has been a keynote speaker for such prestigious corporations and organizations as The Golden Door, Office Depot, Century 21 Real Estate, NAWBO, The Arnold Agency (advertising), and the Ozark Research Institute. She has been interviewed on numerous radio and TV shows all across America since 1995. Jacquelyn feels most honored to have become a highly sought-after advisor to many high-profile authors, entrepreneurs, corporate executives, and healthcare professionals who ALSO desire to make a positive difference in the world.

Prior to her discovery of The 15-Minute ✳ Miracle™, Jacquelyn spent 15 years in the equestrian world practicing the fascinating art of "horse whispering." Before that, she enjoyed training and motivating corporate managers and executives to become the "best of the best" in their respective fields of endeavor. She is absolutely dedicated to finding simple yet practical ways to enable each successive generation to enjoy a higher quality of life than the one before!

Preferred Customer Order Form

To order 15-Minute ✳ Miracle™ books or products, please call 1-(888) In The Flow (that's 1-888-468-4335)
Make checks payable to ♥ Inner Wisdom Publications ✳ PO Box 1341 ✳ Los Gatos, CA 95031-1341

Bill to _____ Home Phone (_____) _____

Address _____

City _____ State _____ Zip _____ Want Playshop Info? Yes ___ No ___

e-mail _____ How did you hear about us? _____

Work phone (_____) _____ Fax (_____) _____ Cell Phone (_____) _____

Cash ____ Check # _____ Visa ____ MC ____ Discover ____ AE ____ Card # _____

Name on the credit card? Same ___ or _____ Expires _____

PO # _____ Comment _____

Date _____ By _____ Sent out _____ Payment received _____ New Customer? Yes ___ No ___

DESCRIPTION	PRICE	QTY.	TOTAL
✳ **DELUXE MIRACLE STARTER KIT** *(items below with a ♥) a $90 Retail Value for only…*	$45.95		$
♥ The 15-Minute ✳ Miracle™ Revealed *(an inspiring "Roadmap to Personal Fulfillment" book)*	17.95		$
♥ Miracle Manifestation Manual *(a "2-Month Journal with Training Wheels & Activities" book)*	19.95		$
♥ Shortcuts to Miracles *(also known as "The Simplified Wisdom Resource Guide")*	9.95		$
♥ Delightful Surprise Gift *(something beautiful to look at and fun to use)*	12.95		$
♥ $30 Gift Certificate *(toward a Personalized Evaluation or Private Consultation with Jacquelyn)*	30.00		$
The 15-Minute ✳ Miracle™ Playbook *(a "Comprehensive Activity Book" to jumpstart your life)*	25.00		
Deluxe ✳ Miracle Attraction Chest™ *(includes over $300 worth of Books, Gifts, and Products)*	199.95		$
Total Prior to Tax, Shipping, and Handling			$
CA residents please add 8% SALES TAX *(subject to change without notice)*			$
SUBTOTAL			
Shipping & Handling Charges $4.95 for each ✳ Deluxe Miracle Starter Kit *(regardless of volume)* $3.95 for the first book on any one order $1.00 x _____ for each additional book $15.00 for Deluxe Miracle Attraction Chest International rates vary *(Please call 1-888-468-4335 or 408-353-2050 for exact total.)* **Total Shipping and Handling**			$ _____
Grand Total in U.S. Funds			$ _____

172